OurTour Guide to Motorhome Morocco

How to Travel Independently to Morocco in Your Motorhome or Campervan

By Julie and Jason Buckley

Second Edition

Copyright 2021 Julie and Jason Buckley

First Published: March 2012

Second Edition: May 2018

Updated: December 2019

Updated: April 2021

Cover photo: Aït Mansour Gorge, Anti-Atlas Mountains, Morocco

Route overview maps used in this book by kind permission of Eric Gaba (Sting - fr:Sting) - Own work Sources of data:SRTM30 Plus; NGDC World Data Bank II (public domain); NGDC GSHHS (public domain); Map Library (public domain)., CC BY-SA 3.0, commons.wikimedia.org/w/index.php?curid=8516904

Maps of Morocco used with permission from © OpenStreetMap contributor, using data available under the Open Database Licence. Please see *openstreetmap.org* for more information.

The authors have made every effort to ensure the accuracy of the information held within this book. However, much of the information given is personal opinion, and no liability can be accepted for errors contained within.

Contents

Introduction 1
Overview Map of Morocco 5
This Second Edition - Things Change 6
Reasons to Travel to Morocco by Motorhome 7
    Because You Can 7
    For the Sheer Adventure 8
    Dramatic Landscapes 10
    The Climate 11
    To Learn About the People and Their Culture 11
    The Infrastructure is in Place 13
    Proximity to Europe 14
    Low Day-to-Day Living Costs 14
    You Don't Need Your Own Motorhome 15
Preparation Before You Go 16
    Preparations for You 16
        Check Foreign Office Advice 16
        Check Your Passports 17
        Vaccinations, Prescriptions and Other Healthcare Issues 18
        Travel Insurance 19
        Guidebooks 19
        Translation Smartphone Application 20
        Bringing Items to Barter or Give Away 20
        Import Restrictions 21
        Read Up to Avoid Offence or Breaking the Law 22
    Preparations for Your Motorhome 24
        V5C and Driving Licenses 24
        Vehicle Insurance and Green Cards 24
        Breakdown Cover in Morocco 24
        Service Your Vehicle 27
        Stock up on LPG or Prepare an Alternative Gas Approach 27
        Maps and GPS Systems 29
        Campsite Books and Databases 30
Taking Your Pet to Morocco 31
    Leaving the UK and Entering the EU 31
    Entering Morocco 33
    Returning from Morocco 34
    Other Pet Considerations 35
    Vets in Morocco 36
Entering Morocco: From Spain to Your First Night Stop 37
    Options for Ferries 37

- Buying Ferry Tickets... 39
- Overnight Parking Before and After the Ferry 42
- Stocking Up on Food and Alcohol – Remember Gibraltar.................. 43
- Catching the Ferry 44
- Passing through the Moroccan Border 46
- First Night's Stop 50
  - Atlantic Coast - Asilah.. 50
  - Mediterranean Coast – Martil.. 51
  - Inland and South East - Chefchaouen 52
  - West – Tangier... 54
- Extending Your 3 Month Visa 54
- Leaving Your Vehicle in Morocco 55

Leaving Morocco: Returning to Spain 56

Driving in Morocco 59
- The Basics – Drive on the Right!... 59
- Navigation 61
- Road Types and Surface Conditions 63
  - Motorways (Autoroutes, A Roads)... 63
  - Major Roads – Shown in Red.. 65
  - Secondary Road – Shown in Yellow... 66
  - Surfaced Roads – White with Solid Lines 67
  - Pistes – White with One side Dashed.. 68
  - Mountain Passes 69
- Getting Around 70
  - Market Days in Towns 71
  - Pedestrians, Donkeys, Traps, Lorries, Bikes and Taxis 71
  - Hitchhikers.. 73
  - Roadworks... 74
  - Fords and Bridges 74
  - Police Road Blocks or Checkpoints.. 75
  - Police Speed Traps.. 76
  - Weather.. 77
  - Dealing with a Breakdown.. 79
  - In the Event of an Accident 80
- Parking.. 81
- Buying Fuel 81
- Using Taxis and Buses.. 82

- Overnight Stays 83
  - Options Available for Motorhome Stopovers 83
    - How to Find Overnight Stops 83
    - Campsites 84
    - Faux Campsites 85
    - Guarded or Guardian Parking 86
    - Free or Wild Camping 87
  - What Standards to Expect 88
    - Price Lists 88
    - Pitches 89
    - Electricity 90
    - Toilets 91
    - Showers 91
    - Grey Water 92
    - Black Water (Toilet Cassette Emptying) 92
    - Fresh Water 92
    - Rubbish Disposal 93
    - Swimming Pools 94
    - On-Site Restaurants 95
    - Clothes Washing 96
    - On-Site Traders 96
    - Leaving Times 97
  - Registering Arrival – Fiches 97
- Some Basics for Day-to-Day Life 97
  - Obtaining Currency – the Moroccan Dirham 98
  - The Many Languages of Morocco 99
  - Insh'Allah 101
  - Guides 102
  - Tourist Information Offices 104
  - Tourist Police 104
  - Accidents 105
  - Swimming in Fresh Water 105
- Shopping 106
  - Buying Food and Drink 106
    - Rough Ideas for Prices 106
    - Supermarkets 106
    - Grocery Shops 107
    - Fruit and Vegetable Shops 107
    - Butchers 108
    - Weekly Souks 110
    - Road-Side Traders 111

- Buying Alcohol 111
- Bartering and Haggling 112
  - What's the Difference? 113
  - The Ethics 113
  - What to Haggle Over, and What Not to 113
  - What to Barter With 116
- Moroccan Regional Specialities 116
- Improvements to Your Motorhome 116

Eating Out 117
- Street Food 118
- Restaurants 119
- Food stalls 119

Staying in Touch with Home 121
- Buying an Internet SIM 121
- Topping up SIM Data 123
- Using your Phone in Morocco 124
- Sending Post 125

Confusions and Annoyances 125
- First Some Perspective 126
- Your Newfound Rockstar Status! 126
- Beggars 127
- Sexual Harassment 129
- Dog Fear and Fascination 129
- Ask the Price First, Always! 130
- The Hard Sell 131
- The False Friend 132
- Motorbike Guides 132
- The False Breakdown 133
- Kif – Drug Dealers in the Rif 133
- Tipping and Baksheesh 134
- Photo Sellers 134
- False Museums 134
- Stone Throwing 135
- Hand Gestures 135
- Taxi Scams 135
- Theft 135

Our Routes 136
- 2012 136
- 2017 138

- Ideas for Places to Visit 141
  - The Atlantic Coast 141
    - Essaouira, Mirleft and Sidi Ifni 141
    - Bird Watching in Moulay Bousselham or the Souss-Massa National Park 145
  - Inland Towns and Cities 147
    - The Imperial Cities – Fes, Meknès and Marrakech 147
    - The Berber Market and Barbary Apes in Azrou 154
    - An Ordinary Town with Extraordinary Hospitality – Bouizakarne 156
  - The Atlas Mountain Ranges 157
    - Waterfall in the Middle Atlas - Cascade d'Ouzoud 157
    - Outstanding Landscapes in the Anti-Atlas – Tafraoute and the Painted Rocks 158
    - High Atlas Mountains - The Tizi-n-Tichka, Aït Benhaddou and the Atlas Film Studios 161
  - Gorges 163
    - The Anti-Atlas Mountain Oasis of the Aït Mansour Gorge 163
    - The Todra and Dadès Gorges 165
  - The South and the Sahara Desert 168
    - The Desert Ring Road – Icht, Tata and Foum Zguid 168
    - The Drâa Valley to the Sahara – Agdz, Zagora and M'hamid 170
    - Parked Alongside Saharan Dunes – Erg Chebbi 173
- About the Authors 175
- Other Books by the Authors 176
- Reference Information 177
  - British Embassy in Rabat 177
  - Useful Websites 177

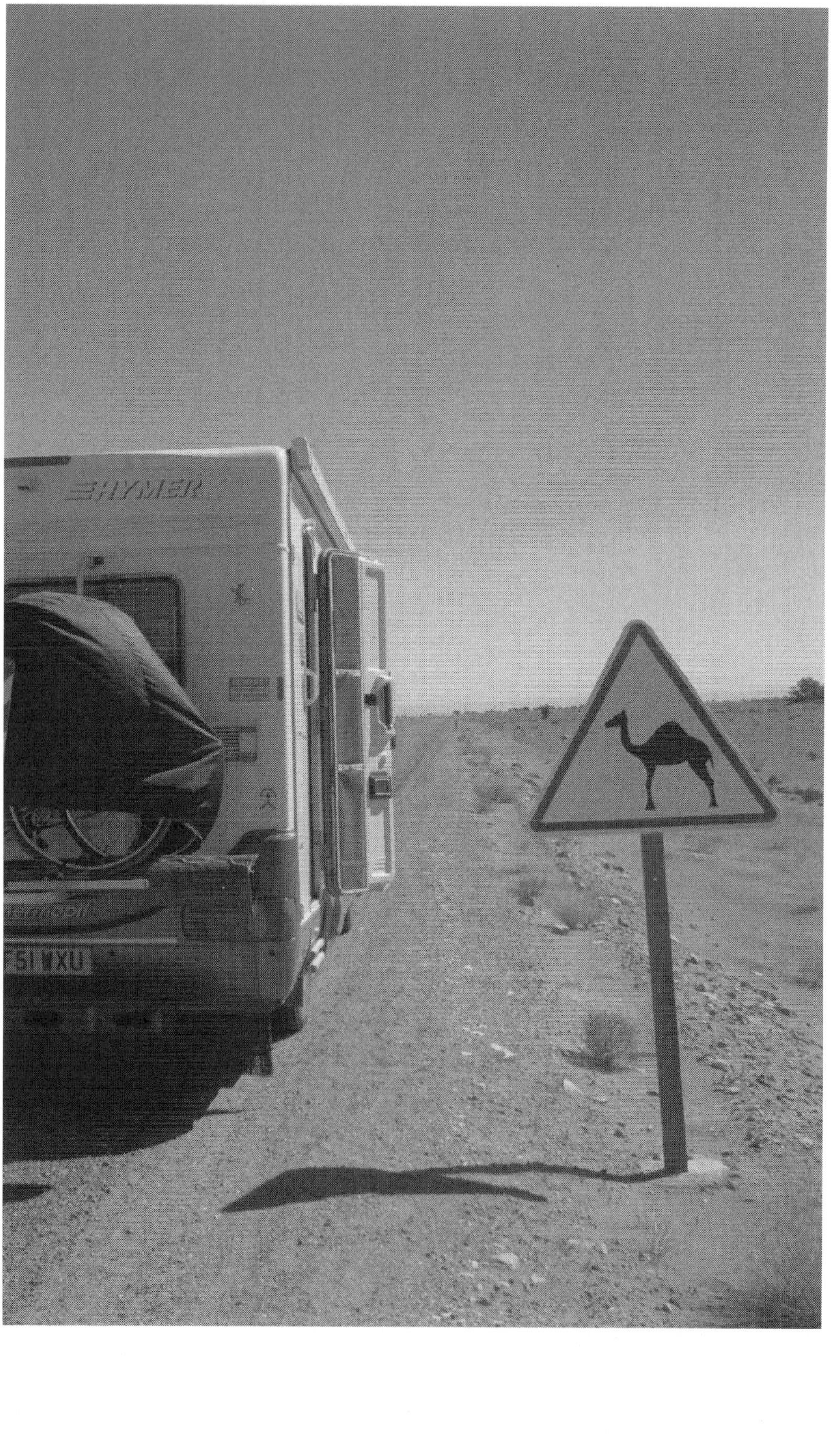
HYMER

Introduction

Morocco is a safe, welcoming and fascinating country to visit by motorhome, and many thousands of vans spend some or all of the winter months here for the great climate, friendly welcome, interesting culture and low cost of living.

Now that the UK has left the EU, Morocco also has the dual advantages of being both (a) outside the Schengen Area and (b) providing free three-month tourist visas at the border. This enables UK residents wanting to spend longer than 90 in 180 days outside the UK to head to Morocco for a few weeks or months to rebuild their Schengen allowance. You could, for example, head to Andalusia in Spain in October, then travel to Morocco in January, return in March and tour Europe, returning to the UK in May, bypassing winter weather completely!

Morocco's extraordinary landscapes, vibrant ancient towns, cool oases, incredible people and movie-set-like deserts of Africa are just a stone's throw away from the southern edge of Europe. At the narrowest point of the Strait of Gibraltar the continents are less than 10 miles apart.

If you fancy it, in the same day you can easily enjoy the hospitality of an English fried breakfast in Gibraltar, and later that same day tuck into a tagine after watching the sunset over the Atlantic from the ramparts of Asilah, south of Tangier in Morocco. If you took a ferry across the Bay of Biscay, and used Spain's fast and free roads to cross the country quickly, you could realistically travel from the UK to Morocco in just a few days, and be sat alongside the edge of the Sahara desert in just a few more.

The Saharan Erg Chebbi, Morocco

We wrote the first edition of this book because we struggled to find information in English when we wanted to take our motorhome and dog to Morocco. After spending a month touring the country independently in our motorhome in January 2012, we'd gathered enough information to help others do the same, so we wrote the book and published it. This second edition was written after spending three months in the country from January to March 2017 and was updated using information from fellow travellers in April 2021.

The Aït Mansour Gorge, Anti-Atlas Mountains, Morocco

Prior to our first tour of Morocco we were very nervous about travelling to the country. We'd also been nervous about driving from France into Spain, for that matter. Our feeling was we weren't experienced enough to complete a trip to Africa, having only spent a couple of months in our 1991 Fiat Ducato Hymer motorhome.

On our second tour we met a couple on the southern Atlantic coast in Morocco, who had bought a new motorhome, having never had one before. They also bought a copy of our book and after reading it had driven directly from the UK across Spain and into Morocco. They were very much enjoying the experience. Our own experience in 2012 was one of feeling stretched, of finding the country both fascinating and confusing. Culture shock hit us hard in the first few days of that tour, but we quickly started to understand something about how the country works, and our place in it.

Our aim with this book is to provide you with enough information to allay any nerves, to give new visitors to Morocco an idea of what to expect on entering the country, and to provide practical help on various aspects of touring independently in a motorhome or campervan. Although Morocco is considered an 'easy introduction to Africa', it isn't Europe, it's far from that. It's a developing, progressive Islamic country, and will immediately feel different to anyone brought up in the Western world.

It seems fairly certain all but the most hardened traveller will experience sights and smells you'd prefer not to in Morocco. But at the same time Morocco is an enthralling place, where each and every day brings something new, some sight you can hardly believe your eyes to see.

Camel racing in the Oued Drâa, Nomad Festival, M'hamid

In feedback to the first edition of this book, one reviewer thanked us and said it swayed him to take a guided tour instead. We're pleased we helped him reach that decision, as he'll enjoy Morocco all the more for doing it his own way. Our choice not to use a guided tour company for any of our North African trips was partly driven by budget, we didn't want to pay around £2000 per tour for a guide.

In the end we found we simply didn't need a tour company, and to us the freedom to travel where and when we wanted was intoxicating. Tour companies have their advantages, offering a sense of security. You can also draw on the experience of your guide to ask questions about the Moroccan way of life, as you're sure to have plenty of them! That said, there are excellent guidebooks available, and you'll find plenty of Moroccans keen to help you find your way around the cities, some of whom speak good English.

Overview Map of Morocco

Morocco is roughly twice the size of the UK and is about the same distance from top to bottom as Norway, around a 1,400-mile drive one way. Most of the country's sights are in the northern half though, along the Atlantic Coast, inland to the Rif Mountains, the Imperial Cities of Fez and Meknes, the Middle Atlas Mountains, the high sand dunes of Erg Chebbi and Erg Chigaga and the oasis towns of the Anti-Atlas Mountains. South of Guelmim lies the Western Sahara region, a vast stony desert which nevertheless attracts hundreds of over-wintering motorhomes for its endless winter sunshine.

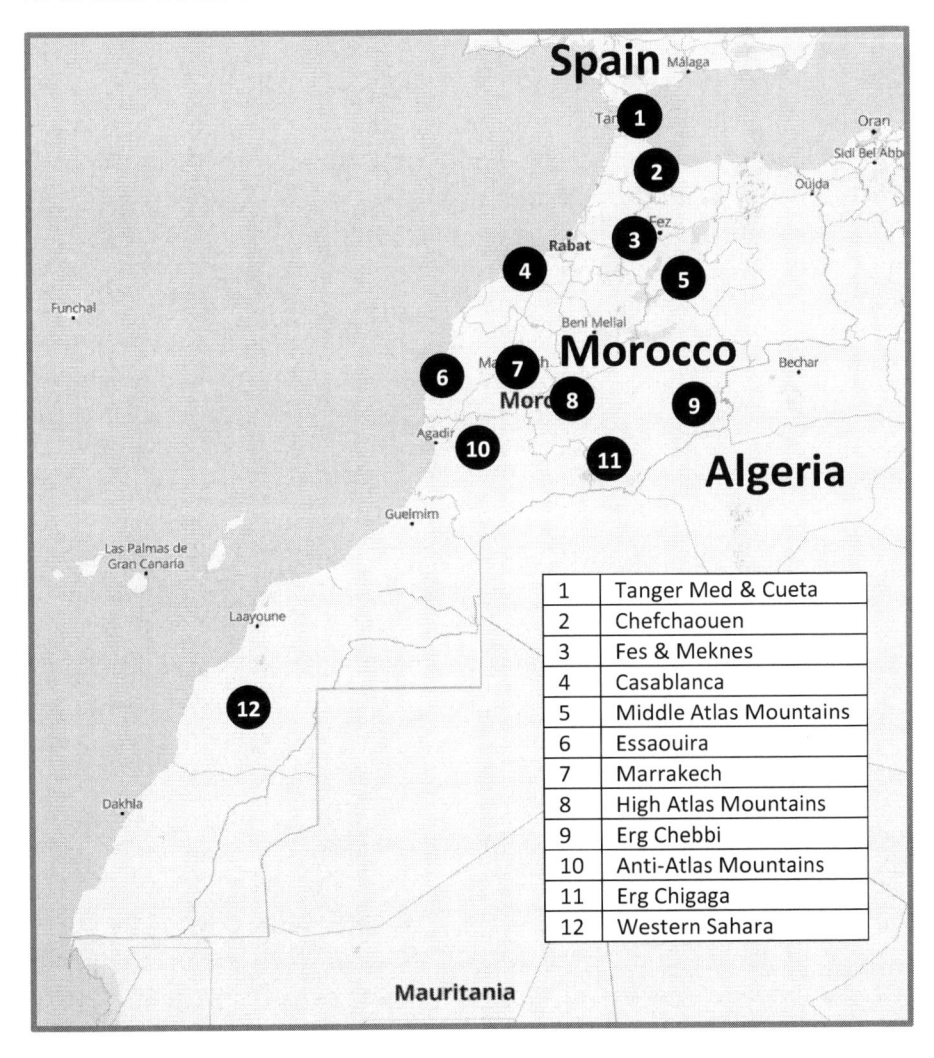

1	Tanger Med & Cueta
2	Chefchaouen
3	Fes & Meknes
4	Casablanca
5	Middle Atlas Mountains
6	Essaouira
7	Marrakech
8	High Atlas Mountains
9	Erg Chebbi
10	Anti-Atlas Mountains
11	Erg Chigaga
12	Western Sahara

This Second Edition - Things Change

We have spent almost six months touring Morocco and Tunisia by motorhome during three separate journeys, staying in roughly 70 locations. These trips have given us hands-on experience of preparing for journeys to North Africa, entering the countries, travelling across them and leaving them. But we must make this point clear: we do not consider ourselves to be in any way experts in either Morocco or travelling by motorhome in Morocco. We remain novices, but that's partly the point of this book: you don't need to be an expert to enjoy a trip like this and, if you don't want to, you don't need to travel with an expert.

In the five-year gap between visits to Morocco we noticed that many things stayed the same, but also that some things changed. There were more campsites and places to stay available, costs had generally gone up, we met far more British motorhome travellers, and more roads had been surfaced. But behind all of that, the country was fundamentally the same, and the roller coaster experience we had in our first visit was just as thrilling second time around.

In late 2019 we brought the book up to date using information from fellow travellers around insurance, the vehicle import process, Internet access, overnight locations and latest costs.

In April 2021 we updated the book again. As well as Brexit the other major change to our world has, of course, been the COVID-19 pandemic. This caused the border between Spain and Morocco to be closed in March 2020. Thousands of motorhomes were stranded in the country until ferries could be organised to take them to back to Europe. From talking to a couple who were staying at a campsite in Sidi Ifni, the Moroccan authorities strictly applied lockdown rules, but treated European motorhome tourists very well for the months they were there awaiting the opportunity to leave.

At the time of writing in April 2021 the Moroccan border is not open to receive tourist traffic from Europe (or the borders are closed to tourists in Europe, so motorhomes can't board ferries to Morocco). Some motorhomes are still in Morocco and the campsites remain accessible. For information on the latest border situation, we'd suggesting checking these sources of information:

- The UK Foreign and Commonwealth Office (FCDO) website: *www.gov.uk/foreign-travel-advice/morocco/entry-requirements*.
- The Maroc-CampingCar French Morocco Motorhome forum (use Google Translate to render into English): *www.maroc-campingcar.com/f4-le-bateau*.
- The route status page of the FRS ferry company: *www.frs.es/en/plan-your-trip/our-routes*.

We've done our best to check the facts presented in this book, but we're not infallible and, as we have said above, things do change. If any aspect of your journey is critical to you, particularly in terms of safety, please double-check the facts elsewhere. This book includes links to various online forums, websites and books to help. If you spot any glaring errors, we'd very much welcome your feedback, by emailing us at julieandjason@ourtour.co.uk, and we'll include them in future editions of the book.

Reasons to Travel to Morocco by Motorhome

Why should you travel to Morocco with your motorhome? While only you can answer that question, of course, here are a few reasons to consider.

Because You Can

COVID-19 aside, thousands upon thousands of motorhome owners travel to Morocco every year. Many of them are retired French couples who have the advantage of speaking fluent French and, since much of Morocco was effectively under French rule for 44 years last century, many locals also speak French. The other advantage they have is the availability of high-quality French language books and forums for travelling in Morocco. That aside, they have no special knowledge which you can't easily acquire yourself, from reading this book and the other reference material we suggest.

Some of the thousands of motorhomes in Morocco (Camping Tazerzite near Tiznit)

If you can drive your motorhome in Europe, and are comfortable boarding a ferry, then you have the basic skills you need to visit Morocco. There are, however, some special circumstances which you are likely to only come across in Morocco, and this book aims to help prepare you for them. As the locals say "you Europeans may have watches, but we Moroccans have time". All you need to do when you come across something unusual is take your time, use your common sense, and you'll (at least in hindsight!) enjoy overcoming it.

For the Sheer Adventure

The first time we parked our old Hymer against the high, wind-sculptured dunes of the Erg Chebbi, the hairs on our arms stood up in awe and excitement. We'd just driven to the Sahara. Us! With no-one guiding us, no-one reassuring us they'd take care of the unknown, we were stood alongside our trusty two-wheel drive Fiat, feeling like we'd driven straight through the TV screen and into a film set. We couldn't quite believe we were there and felt both elated and proud of what we'd achieved.

Us at Erg Chebbi, north of Merzouga, in 2012

We've felt the same elation a number of times across our two tours. Looking out over the frenetic Djeema el-Fna square from the balcony of Café de France in Marrakech. Standing in the ancient ksar of Aït Benhaddou north of Ouarzazate, which has been used as a set for Gladiator among many other films. Staring out from the top of a boulder-strewn hill in Tafraoute in the Anti-Atlas Mountains. Driving the narrow road through the Aït Mansour mountain oasis, the fronds of palms brushing our van sides and the high orange cliff sides visible through the sunroof. Propping our feet on the van dashboard, with sunlight streaming across surfers bobbing about in the crashing waves of the Atlantic at Sidi Ifni. It's a long list.

Dramatic Landscapes

Morocco's landscapes vary enormously. Along the coastlines you will find long stretches of beach and nature reserves, while the north of the country is relatively mild and green. A series of mountain ranges cross the country from the south-west to the north-east, the high peaks of the High Atlas, the lower Middle Atlas and the jaw-dropping combed rock of the Anti-Atlas.

Travelling east, once you're over the mountains, the land becomes rapidly arid, and you'll find yourself crossing huge swathes of *hamada* – stony desert, until you eventually reach one of Morocco's two Saharan *ergs*, high dunes of butter-coloured fine sand. In the south the Anti-Atlas mountain landscape is also dry, presenting a variety of backdrops made up from enormous boulders, or rocky hillsides worn into sweeping layers. The exploding green tops of palm trees fill the creases in the hills, giving away the hidden streams of water magically appearing from underground rivers to create life in the oases.

A camel eyeing us up in the Anti-Atlas Mountains

The Climate

Around the southern Atlantic coastal town of Agadir, the campsites are packed in the winter with thousands of motorhomes. Why are they there? Well, perhaps because it's sunny, warm and dry, all winter. The average daily highs are around 20°C, even in December and January. Nighttime averages fall to 8°C though, so you may want to bring an electric heater to keep the chill off! Down this far south the sun shines for an average of about seven hours per day through the winter, not bad at all.

Other parts of the country can get very cold in winter, particularly in the mountains. We've driven past snow several times when in the Middle Atlas Mountains and were once unable to move campsites as the snow gates were closed along the road.

Snow in the Middle Atlas

To Learn About the People and Their Culture

Morocco's population is reputed to be between 93% and 99% Muslim, depending on which statistics you believe, and the country is governed under policies anchored in Islam. The current regent, who is effectively in charge of the country, is King Mohammed VI. You'll see photographs of him everywhere, and he has a claim to be a direct descendant of the Prophet Muhammad.

The culture of Morocco is therefore deeply entwined with Islam, which was first apparent to us within hours of arrival, when we were caught out by the sing-song *adhan*, the call to prayer ringing out like a siren from the loudspeakers of an adjacent mosque's minaret.

Morocco is a developing country by Western standards. Millions of people live on miniscule amounts of money. *www.minimum-wage.org* gives the legal minimum wage of agriculture workers as around £5.60 per day. Women in rural towns stand knee-deep in cold streams or irrigation channels, washing clothes by hand, or walk bent double for miles on end, along roads through the stony deserts carrying heavy loads of sticks. Men shout at horses or mules as they struggle to work a field using an ancient wooden plough. Hushed stories of corruption and class discrimination faced by the poor of the population bring flushes of anger. The poverty and hardships are clear to see, and the Moroccans bear them with dignity.

A young baker in the Fes medina

According to the World Bank (*data.worldbank.org*), 26% of the population aged over 15 were illiterate in 2018. Although this sounds bad, the illiteracy rate was 33% just ten years ago, and 58% in 1994, so it's reducing fairly quickly. Morocco is changing. The most obvious physical evidence of change is Tanger Med port, a huge modern facility where you may well arrive in the country. Opened in 2007, Tanger Med is the largest port in Africa with a total capacity of nine million shipping containers a year.

Another indication of change in the five-year gap between our two tours was the rapidly-improving conditions of the roads. The Michelin map we used for navigation in 2012 showed long stretches of road to be *piste* (packed mud and rock), which has since been smoothed and sealed with tarmac. A new motorway has also appeared, running across from Casablanca to Beni Mellal, which wasn't even shown as being planned on the old map.

Despite these modern additions, Morocco and many of the Moroccan people remain stubbornly, well, Moroccan. A French couple we met in Marrakech who'd lived and travelled in Morocco for 20 years told us they'd seen many changes in that time, but it takes longer than 20 years to change the Moroccans. Trying to describe quite what makes the Arabs and Berbers of Morocco who they are, their psyche, their open approach to strangers of all faiths, their view of family life, their approach to work, the way they deal with daily difficulties, the way in which they share their housing and transport, their craftsmanship, their music and much more, is simply beyond us. You really need to travel to Morocco and see for yourself.

The Infrastructure is in Place

Morocco's road network is easily capable of carrying a two-wheel drive European motorhome or campervan to the far edges of the country. An ever-expanding, high quality toll motorway network enables you to leave the port at Tanger Med and drive all the way to Agadir, 500 miles away, without leaving it. The country has a good spread of established campsites, which have been welcoming motorhomes for years and are well used to our needs. There are European-style supermarkets positioned around the larger towns and cities, with fixed prices, good quality food and spacious car parks. If you wanted to, you could almost (but not quite) travel across Morocco without really knowing you were there. That would be a real shame of course, but the level to which you immerse yourself in the country is up to you.

Part of the Moroccan autoroute (motorway) network

Proximity to Europe

At only ten miles away Morocco is closer to Spain than Calais is to Dover, and you can easily see Africa from Gibraltar. The ferry route we used from Algeciras in Spain to the modern Tanger Med port takes only 60 to 90 minutes (although you may need to allow a few hours waiting time either side of the crossing!). There are also longer routes available from Barcelona, France and Italy if you want to cut out some or all the drive across Spain.

Low Day-to-Day Living Costs

Although costs aren't likely to be the biggest factor in anyone's decision to visit a country, it is useful to have an idea, especially if you're on a tight budget. Wild camping isn't widely accepted across most of Morocco (the far south being a notable exception), so it is best to budget for overnight costs, especially for first time visitors. We visited a range of campsites and other types of parking location, and only free camped for two nights. As of late 2020, the price for a campsite pitch ranged from around 120Dh, £10 a night for a high-quality campsite outside Marrakech (for two people, including electricity, on a site which rivals European standards), down to £1.20 for a basic municipal parking area in Tafraoute. As a very broad rule of thumb, campsites are about £6 a night without electricity, or £8 with electricity.

In 2012 our 30-day tour cost us £1269, around £42 per day, which included these major items:

- Ferry tickets: £153 (€180)
- Vehicle insurance: £78
- Internet access: £15
- Diesel: £170 - 1830 miles
- Campsite fees: £212
- Eating out most days, with the odd alcoholic drink: £255
- Supermarket food: £135

In 2017, our 90-day tour costs worked out at £1960, around £22 per day, which included these major items:

- Ferry tickets: £170 (€200)
- Vehicle insurance: £0 (free Green Card provided with yearly insurance)
- Internet access: £30
- Diesel: £321 - 3992 miles
- Campsite fees: £560 (average £6.22 per night)
- Eating out occasionally: £268
- Supermarket food: £467

As of early 2021, ferry tickets are roughly the same price, but expect some of the other costs to be higher than those above, specifically a Green Card from your motorhome insurer which might cost in the region of £200 to £500. We'll come back to this later in the book.

You Don't Need Your Own Motorhome

We took our own motorhome when we visited Morocco, but you don't have to. We saw several motorhomes across the country from Zigzag Camper (*www.zigzagcamper.com*), a hire company based just north of Marrakech. There may be more companies that offer this service too, but with fewer logos on their campers so we didn't spot them. We don't know what the service is like, but if you don't own a motorhome or you don't fancy taking your own, this could be an option to consider.

Preparation Before You Go

Before setting out from Europe, here are some things to check for you and your motorhome, to ensure you have a smooth visit to Morocco.

Preparations for You

Check Foreign Office Advice

At the time of writing the UK Foreign and Commonwealth Development Office (FCDO) advises against any international travel due to the COVID-19 pandemic (*www.gov.uk/foreign-travel-advice*). This means that many travel insurance policies won't be valid for travel to Morocco (or anywhere else) but doesn't in itself make it illegal to travel there. As vaccination rates increase during 2021 FCDO advice may change, so we can only advise keeping a close eye on the website and the news when planning your future tours.

Prior to COVID-19, the events in the winter of 2010 were perhaps the biggest area the FCDO might have been concerned about. These events precipitated the Arab Spring which took place in 2011, which saw the leadership of numerous North African and Middle Eastern countries toppled. Morocco wasn't left untouched. Although the King remained in power, he was forced to enact various reforms as a result of what was happening to the east. Since then the country's leadership has remained strong. While many other countries in the region found themselves struggling with internal conflict and terrorism, Morocco has escaped largely unscathed in this respect.

We've had no issues with regards to being made to feel unwelcome or feeling at risk of attack in any way. That said, situations change, and it makes sense to check out the advice from your country's foreign office before travelling.

However, it is best to take this advice in context. At the time of writing in April 2021 the UK foreign office website states "terrorists are very likely to try to carry out attacks in Morocco", and reminds us of an attack which took place in 2018: "Two foreign nationals were murdered while hiking near Mount Toubkal in December 2018". This sounds terrible and could force you to put your plans on hold or to visit France or Spain instead.

But take a moment to check out what the same site says for France: "terrorists are very likely to try to carry out attacks in France.", or Spain "terrorists are likely to try to carry out attacks in Spain". In these times when terrorism can and does strike anywhere, it can be very confusing, especially if you read any of the uninformed banter on forums from people who have never been to Morocco. Make your own decision and if you are still uncertain, speak to people who have recently visited the country.

Check Your Passports

British visitors to Morocco are issued with a three-month visa upon arriving in the country, so there is no need to apply for a visa. This time can be extended to six months within any 12 months once you're in the country, as outlined later. For UK passport holders, the UK Foreign Office site states the passport needs to be valid for the duration of your time in the country, however other sites state that six month's validity from the date of entering the country is needed.

It may be that this is the case only for those people from countries who need to apply for a visa before entering Morocco. To be safe and reduce stress levels, it would make sense to have at least six month's validity on all of your passports at the point you enter the country. When the UK leaves the EU, passports will also need a minimum of six months validity and need to be less than ten years old.

You will also need a free page in your passport for entry and exit stamps, and vehicle import reference numbers to be stamped in it by the Moroccan authorities.

Vaccinations, Prescriptions and Other Healthcare Issues

The UK NHS (*www.fitfortravel.nhs.uk*) suggests that you visit your GP six to eight weeks before travelling to Morocco, to:

- Confirm your primary courses and boosters are up to date "including for example, seasonal flu vaccine (if indicated), MMR, vaccines required for occupational risk of exposure, lifestyle risks and underlying medical conditions"
- Receive recommended courses or boosters: Hepatitis A; Tetanus
- Consider other vaccines: Rabies, Typhoid
- Selectively advised vaccines - only for those individuals at highest risk: Hepatitis B.

Malaria isn't normally present in Morocco, and no yellow fever vaccination certificate is needed. We didn't realise any of this, and so we did none of the above checks, and neither of us were ill. That said, now that we know we should, we'll pop and see our GPs before we visit Morocco again.

If you're travelling with prescription medication, the UK Foreign Office suggests "if you will be travelling with medication (including over the counter medication) you should check for any restrictions on medications before you travel, you can do this by contacting the embassy of the country you're visiting."

It's also worth stocking up with a decent sunscreen (we used Factor 50 most days, even in winter) and mosquito repellent. While we didn't get bitten once in our four months of travel in Morocco, we met a British mother-daughter couple who got quite badly bitten overnight in a beachside resort south of Essaouira after watching TV with the motorhome door open at dusk. Other than dealing with the bites they were fine, but the NHS website states that there is Dengue Fever, a viral illness transmitted by mosquito bites, in the country. There is no vaccine, so the only prevention is to avoid mosquito bites.

Travel Insurance

The EHIC and new UK-issued GHIC (Global Health Insurance Card) cards aren't valid in Morocco. Taking out suitable travel insurance is recommended by pretty much everyone. Policies and insurers change quickly, so while we've mentioned a couple of insurers below, we can't recommend a specific company. We can suggest you think about the following when buying insurance:

- Since the start of the COVID-19 pandemic, only selected insurers will issue policies for countries which the UK FCDO (Foreign Office) recommends against travelling to due to the disease. Some of them won't cover you for the effects of COVID-19 itself (for example: *truetraveller.com*), while others cover any impact on the disease itself too (for example: *heymondo.com*). Check the policy wording carefully and ask the company directly any questions you have.
- Ensure the policy covers Morocco, and any 'unusual activities' you may want to take part in, including skiing (yes, you can ski in Morocco), quad biking or camel trekking.
- If you're on a long trip (over a year) many companies won't issue a policy unless you've been living in the UK for six of the previous 12 months.
- Check how long you can be back in the UK for during the policy for it to remain valid. We took out a two-year policy and could return to the UK twice for a maximum of 21 days.

Guidebooks

During our two tours of Morocco we used an old copy of Lonely Planet Morocco (the latest paperback version is available from Amazon UK for £9.48). This proved very useful for background information but being 15 years old it was dated even without taking into account prices and restaurant reviews! The other two guidebooks fellow travellers were using were DK Eyewitness Travel Guide Morocco (paperback from £12.28 from *amazon.co.uk*), and The Rough Guide to Morocco (paperback from £10.07 from Amazon UK). These both looked excellent, although the Eyewitness Guide was more focussed on visuals than textual information. All the books are available as eBooks too, if you want to save space in your motorhome.

Translation Smartphone Application

If you have a smartphone, you may want to consider installing a translation application while you have a WiFi network available. We installed Google Translate, which is free and proved very useful. This includes the option to download 'offline' translation packs for various languages. We downloaded French and Arabic and found ourselves using the Arabic pack to communicate with locals, who spoke no French, as they helped us when we broke down. On some phones you can also start the app and point the phone's camera at French signs, menus, forms and so on, and it'll do a passable job of showing you the translation on the screen.

Bringing Items to Barter or Give Away

Moroccans will make good use of items which we in Europe will discard as worthless, or next to worthless. Old clothes – especially children's and baby clothes, push bikes, tools, out-of-date phones and other electronics seem to be in highest demand, but pretty much anything will be wanted in many places. It's worth looking around your home before you leave, or your motorhome while you're on the road, for things you don't use and are willing to swap for local goods or give away.

On our first trip we bartered a push bike and child trailer, hot water bottle, wind-up radio and various other items for a coat, two blankets and a silk throw. On our second trip we took an old iPhone and iPad, plus the charging cable and gave them away to a Berber family we met who were working hard to build a campsite. It's important to note that we didn't give items away to children begging, there's more about this issue later.

Import Restrictions

When entering Morocco, you can't freely bring anything you like into the country. The website for the Moroccan Passport and Visa services gives a list of what you can and cannot bring (*morocco.visahq.com/customs*). A few personal observations about this:

- Technically you cannot import (or export) Moroccan currency (the Dirham). In practice no-one checked us at either stage, and our friends changed a small amount of Dirhams in Gibraltar back to Euros. Some sources state the authorities tolerate up to 1000 Dirhams. If you travel into Morocco via the Tanger Med port, there are a number of currency exchange booths just after customs and a cashpoint, or you could just drive to your destination town, avoiding the toll roads as they only take cash, and use a cash machine there, nearly every town has one.
- The import laws around alcohol are widely flouted by motorhome travellers. We aren't suggesting you do the same, or condoning breaking the law, just reporting our observations. Technically only a litre of alcohol is allowed, but we witnessed many motorhomes with their own personal wine cellar in the garage, well stocked and well used during months in the sunshine. As noted in a later chapter, the border checks were minimal on our entries into Morocco – there was no need to be hiding beer cans in the fresh water tank...

Read Up to Avoid Offence or Breaking the Law Although Morocco is physically close to Spain, even sharing a land border with it in places, it's a million miles away in terms of customs and the law. The UK Foreign Office has a section on local laws and customs which it is worth referring to (*www.gov.uk/foreign-travel-advice/morocco/local-laws-and-customs*). At the time of writing, the advice could be summarised as follows:

1. Avoid public displays of affection. Don't hold hands with your partner while in public, or have your arm around their shoulders. Don't kiss your partner in public. Don't hug in public. We found this difficult, no touching each other at all while outside the van, but if you look at the locals very few of them break these social rules.
2. Sexual relations outside marriage, and homosexuality, are both illegal. Travelling in a motorhome grants a degree of privacy not available if you're having to check into hotels, for example. Nevertheless, it would make sense not to advertise either of these in public.
3. Virginity at marriage is still of critical importance in Morocco, leading to a degree of frustration in young men which is directed in particular towards Western women, especially those travelling alone. The importance of dressing highly conservatively can't be over-stated, especially away from the more Western-influenced cities. Women should cover everything but their hair, faces and hands while in public, and avoid any tight-fitting clothing. Men should cover everything but their hair, faces, hands and forearms. Men should ideally wear buttoned shirts rather than T shirts, which are seen as underwear in some more remote places. You'll see plenty of motorhome travellers breaking these rules, wearing shorts and strappy tops which are absolutely the norm in Europe, but seen as shocking to some Moroccans. The way in which the locals perceive you, and the degree of resect they afford to you, will be at least in part driven by the amount of respect you show to their customs.

4. Although Morocco has a fairly liberal view of alcohol, it is sold in some shops, licensed restaurants and a few supermarkets, and some locals will ask you for wine, beer or whiskey, it is forbidden under Islam. The locals won't openly drink alcohol in public and will expect you not to either.
5. Check whether you will be in Morocco during Ramadan. If you are, you should take note of the special etiquette it brings with it, such as not eating or smoking in public during the day.
6. Despite the open availability of some drugs, in particular marijuana in the Rif Mountains, they are illegal for possession, use or sale.
7. It is illegal to send passports through the post.
8. It is illegal to possess pornographic material.
9. It is illegal to possess bibles in Arabic, or to take part in any activity which attempts to convert Muslims to other religions.
10. You need special permission to import or fly drones in Morocco (see *www.drone-made.com/post/morocco-drone-laws for more details*).

Note: campsites and tourist hotels and restaurants are something of a special case for these guidelines. Treat them on a case by case basis, but within their walls you can often get away with more 'European behaviour' than outside. For example, wearing shorts and drinking alcohol outside (as long as you're out of sight of a mosque) is often tolerated.

Preparations for Your Motorhome

V5C and Driving Licenses

In order to temporarily import your vehicle into Morocco, you'll need the original copy of your V5C registration certificate (not a photocopy). The Moroccans refer to this with its French name of *carte grise* (pronounced cart greez). You'll also need your EU driving license card (or licenses if you have multiple drivers) in case you're stopped by the police. When we were stopped the police were only interested in the EU photo card (the paper part hasn't been in use since 2015 anyway). There is no need for an International Driving Permit.

Vehicle Insurance and Green Cards

It's unlikely your normal insurance policy will cover you for Morocco, so ideally you will need your provider to issue you with a Green Card, which extends your insurance cover to other countries. Some companies may charge for this service, while others may refuse to issue a Green Card, which is why you should consider your trip to Morocco before you take out or renew your policy, so you can switch providers if necessary.

Breakdown Cover in Morocco

The road from M'hamid, on the northern edge of the Sahara

On trips to Morocco we were members of the German breakdown organisation ADAC (*www.adac.de*). This is the German equivalent of the AA, but they're no longer taking new non-German customers. They cover

Morocco to a degree but the precise level of cover they offer in Morocco remained a slight mystery though. From the terms it appeared they would cover the motorhome in Morocco for up to 92 days but would only reimburse costs up to specified levels and they wouldn't send out a breakdown truck.

It's obvious when you're in the country that there is no national network of breakdown vehicles like the AA or RAC, but instead a collection of locally-managed breakdown vehicles and mechanics. With that in mind, we worked on the assumption that if we broke down in Morocco, we'd be largely on our own, although we knew we'd have support from fellow motorhome travellers also in Morocco at the same time as us.

Tour companies for Morocco offer help in the event of a breakdown, which is perhaps the single biggest reason we might be tempted to buy a tour. In the end we opted to avoid the high cost (and fixed itinerary) of an escorted tour and we only 'broke down' once and took care of it ourselves, as described later in the book.

The Green Card only proves you have the legal minimum insurance to travel in the countries it applies to. If you have comprehensive insurance check with your insurer what level of cover applies to the Green Card countries. If you can't get a Green Card from your provider you can buy third-party insurance at the Moroccan border, but it can be quite expensive and won't cover damage to your vehicle.

Note: if you also have a moped, motorbike or quad bike, you need to ensure you have the legal level of cover for them too while in Morocco, either from your UK insurer or by buying insurance in Morocco.

On our first visit to Morocco our insurer refused to issue a Green Card, so we bought third party insurance at the Tanger Med port after passing through customs. The Moroccan insurance cost us 950 Dirhams, which was about £80 (€92), for one month's stay. The agent initially tried to charge us around £220 (€260) which we refused to pay, pointing out that we had a caravan, not a commercial van (our first taste of buying in Morocco!). The agent issued us with a certificate, but there was no kind of policy booklet, so it wasn't clear what the terms of the cover were. Buying at the border placed us at risk, since we didn't know the terms of the policy. In July 2020 a motorhome owner in Morocco reported they paid £190 for 3 months 'border insurance'.

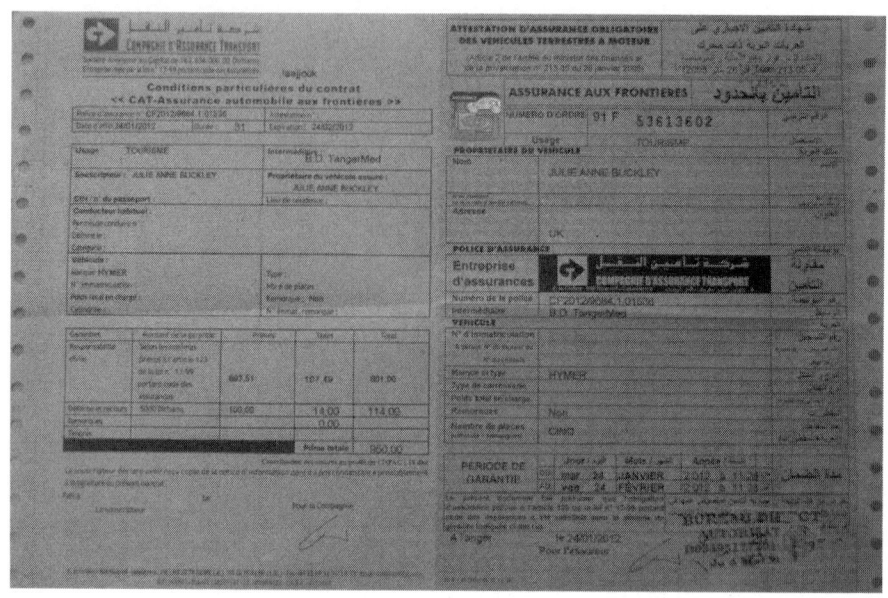

Insurance document issued at Tanger Med

Before our second trip, at insurance renewal, we switched to a provider who would issue a Green Card, as well as cover us for 365 days of travel in Europe. They posted us an A4 sheet which states the dates the Green Card is valid for, and has a list of countries it covers, including MA, Morocco (in this case it listed more countries than were covered, but these were crossed out). As we didn't know exactly when we would be traveling to Morocco, our provider made the Green Card valid for the same dates as the underlying policy, a full year, but some insurers insist you provide specific dates for your time in Morocco. As of April 2021, insurers being reported as offering Green Cards include:

- Comfort (*www.comfort-insurance.co.uk*)
- Saga (over 50s only - *www.saga.co.uk*)
- Herts Insurance (*www.hertsinsurance.com*)
- Sterling (*www.sterling-insurance.co.uk*)
- Victor Milwell (*www.vminsurance.co.uk*)
- Adrian Flux (*www.adrianflux.co.uk*)
- Advance Insurance Brokers (*advanceinsurance.co.uk*)

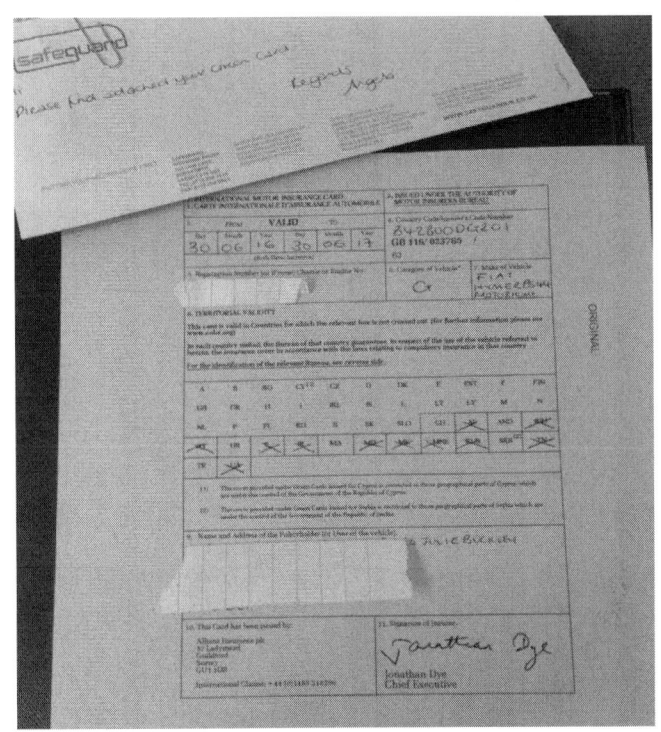

A Green Card for Morocco. Note that the 'MA' box must not be crossed out

Service Your Vehicle

It's probably stating the obvious, but if you're planning to drive to Morocco it makes a lot of sense to ensure your vehicle's in sound mechanical condition, including the tyres. Mechanics in Morocco have a reputation for being able to fix anything, and for a reasonable price, but enjoyment of our tours was certainly higher when we didn't break down! Also note that you need to carry a warning triangle in case of breakdowns in Morocco.

Stock up on LPG or Prepare an Alternative Gas Approach

Morocco uses the French style of gas bottle, so you can't simply swap a UK Calor bottle for one of these. If you have a self-refillable LPG system, then note that there are no LPG refill stations in Morocco, including the Spanish enclaves at Ceuta and Melilla. If you are taking a ferry from Algeciras, www.mylpg.eu indicates there are two LPG stations near to the port, and it makes sense to top up before leaving for Morocco:

1. Repsol Los Barios, on the A381 north-west of Algeciras (GPS: N36.199923, W5.514737)
2. Codes, just off the A7 between Algeciras and Gibraltar (GPS: N36.204136, W5.412049)

It is, obviously, hard to estimate exactly how much gas you'll need for a tour of Morocco. As a very (very) rough guide, we used 20 litres (about 10Kg) of gas during our 3-month tour in January to March. During normal winter touring in Europe, we'd use more gas but in Morocco we spent most of our time on campsites and paid for electrical hook-up in order to limit our gas consumption. We used an electric fan heater for heating, an electric kettle for hot water, an electric hob for cooking and we ran our fridge on electricity. Hook-up is normally an additional charge on campsites, between 20 and 30 Dirhams a night (£1.60 to £2.40).

There are other gas options in addition to preserving your European-bought supply, these include:

1. Buy a local Moroccan bottle and pigtail (the high-pressure hose which connects the bottle to your regulator), and-connect it in your gas locker. Moroccan gas bottles are generally very well 'used', so you may want to take care choosing a bottle to avoid buying a heavily damaged one. It is worth noting that Moroccan gas has a reputation for being 'dirty', especially butane. We have no direct experience of this since we relied on Spanish LPG, but we were contacted by two other British motorhomes who were using Moroccan propane with no issues.
2. Another option if you have refillable LPG would be to use a Moroccan bottle sat beside your motorhome, connected with a high-pressure hose direct to your LPG refill point, sold by an LPG system supplier. We met one British motorhome using this solution without problems. Again, the risk of 'dirty gas' remains, and you need to carry the spare bottle inside the van when you travel.
3. There are a handful of gas refill plants across Morocco who will reportedly refill your LPG bottles for you if you remove them from your van first. We've not been able to confirm the existence of any of these plants though.

4. We also heard reports of campsites around Agadir offering to refill gas bottles for you. We saw this taking place once; one gas bottle in a tree in the sun, poured into another on the floor in the shade, and decided against trying it!

Maps and GPS Systems

The most widely used road map of Morocco is the Michelin National 742. Get the latest version you can, as the road improvements mean that they are quickly out of date. They cost about £6 from Amazon UK, but if you wait until you reach Morocco it will cost you a bit more and may be an older version (ours cost £8.50 in 2012, from a Moroccan petrol station and had a fine layer of dust on it).

While the Michelin Map is great for planning and navigating your way across the country, it's not good for finding your way around towns. The first time we visited Morocco we paid around £30 for the TomTom Morocco map, but at the time it was incomplete and inaccurate. We have spoken to people who bought their satnav map more recently and had no problems with it, however we have found that free and better solutions are now available.

Navigating between towns is fairly easy, lots of long roads!

During our 2017 tour we used the free *maps.me* application, which runs on various types of mobile device. We downloaded the maps for Morocco onto each device while we had a WiFi connection in Spain, and after that the maps did not need an Internet connection to work. *Maps.me* will work out routes for you, which we used in conjunction with our Michelin Map. It has accurate and useful maps, as well as many points of interest such as campsites, supermarkets and car parks, but it was understandably a little clueless when it came to estimating journey times. If you've a good enough Internet connection and data allowance then Google Maps (*google.co.uk/maps*) also provides coverage for Morocco, although we've never tested its results.

Campsite Books and Databases

There are a large number of established campsites across Morocco, but the quality of them varies enormously, and some areas of the country have sparse facilities. The most complete, comprehensive and up to date campsite book we found was *Campings du Maroc* by J. Gandini (£33 from Amazon UK for the 2020/21 Edition), but it's only available in French and as a paperback book.

We found website databases to be a great alternative to books. These cover Moroccan campsites and other types of overnight parking and have an application (app) which can be downloaded to your smartphone or tablet when you have WiFi, so you can search the database even when you don't have an Internet connection. You can also see reviews from fellow travellers who have recently visited the campsites, making the databases always up to date. At the time of writing, the best of these is (arguably) *campercontact.com*. The offline copy costs around £5 per year, or if you have Internet access you can browse the *campercontact.com* website for free.

Other websites (which also have offline applications) to check out are: *park4night.com* (English), *ioverlander.com* (English) and *campingcar-infos.com* (French). Many of the databases allow point of interest (POI) downloads too, so you can load up all of the locations into your satnav to make selecting your destination easier during route planning.

Taking Your Pet to Morocco

You can take your pet cats, dogs or ferrets (as long as they're over 12 weeks old) to Morocco. Our dog Charlie visited the country twice and loved snuffling up any dates that had fallen off the palm trees. While we can give you information from first-hand experience of being in Morocco with your dog, we're far from being experts on the laws around pet travel and spent time checking the rules and talking to our vet before we took Charlie there. The requirements of pet travel for the UK, EU and Morocco change from time to time, as they have following Brexit, plus your pet may have specific requirements we're not aware of. We strongly recommend discussing your travel plans with your vet a few months before travelling if possible.

Leaving the UK and Entering the EU

As of 1 January 2021, the EU Pet Passport has been replaced with Animal Health Certificates (AHCs) in Great Britain. Northern Ireland has retained the Pet Passport (*www.nidirect.gov.uk/articles/taking-your-pets-abroad*), so if you live in Northern Ireland and have an EU Pet Passport issued by a vet from NI, you can continue to use it for travel to the UK, the EU and Morocco.

AHCs allow pets to be taken into the EU and returned to the UK without having to go into quarantine. The certificate is valid for your pet to stay abroad within the EU for up to four months, and at the time of writing it is unclear if you will be able get a new AHC while abroad, enabling you to prolong your trip or if you will have to return to the UK to get a new one. We recommend you talk to you vet and check the latest government information on the AHCs, available here: *www.gov.uk/guidance/pet-travel-to-europe-from-1-january-2021*.

To obtain an AHC, you'll need to complete these steps:

1. You must have your dog, cat or ferret microchipped.
2. A vet must vaccinate your dog, cat or ferret against rabies, and your pet must be at least 12 weeks old before it can be vaccinated.
3. You must wait 21 days after the primary vaccination before travel.
4. You must visit your British vet to get an AHC for your pet, no more than 10 days before travel to the EU.

Each AHC is valid for:

1. Up to five pets.
2. 10 days after the date of issue for entry into the EU or NI.
3. Onward travel within the EU or NI for 4 months after the date of issue.
4. Re-entry to Great Britain for 4 months after the date of issue.

As you plan to travel to an 'unlisted country' (Morocco), you'll also need your vet to test that the rabies vaccination has worked (a rabies antibody titration test) and provide written proof. This test has to be done 'least 30 days after the date of vaccination and not less than three months before the date of movement' (which we believe to be the date that you will return to the EU from Morocco).

> You can read the official conditions around bringing a pet back into the EU here: ec.europa.eu/food/animals/pet-movement/eu-legislation/non-commercial-non-eu_en

Before going abroad make sure your pet's yearly vaccination booster jabs are all up to date. While you can easily get them done abroad, you may want to bring them forward and get your own vet to do them (especially the rabies vaccination, because it's only valid for one year if done in some parts of Europe).

At the time of writing in April 2021, it doesn't appear possible for a British resident to use an AHC issued in Britain to enter Morocco, and then use it to return to the EU and back into the UK. Some British residents are reporting on forums they are working around the limitations of the AHC by obtaining an EU Pet Passport from a vet located in the EU, in Portugal, Spain or France for example. This is the approach we'd personally look to take, removing the need to keep buying AHCs for every trip, removing the 4-month limit on travel, and making a return from Morocco to Spain simple. It would mean that future vaccinations would have to be carried out in the EU though, something we'd have to plan for if we wanted to keep the EU Pet Passport valid. We'd also need to remember the need for written evidence of a test confirming the initial rabies vaccination worked.

We've also seen media reports that the UK continues to discuss 'Part 1 Listed' status with the EU. If this is granted in the future, then UK-based vets will be able to issue UK pet passports, which would avoid the need for an AHC each time you travel or to obtain a new EU Pet Passport abroad. Something to keep an eye out for in the media or talk to you vet about.

Entering Morocco

To enter Morocco, your pet officially needs a valid Pet Passport or AHC (and therefore needs to comply with the requirements to obtain the passport – microchip, rabies vaccination and so on). Technically you also need a Veterinary Certificate, dated less than eight days from the date of entry into Morocco, stating that your pets are in good health. In our case we entered Morocco twice at Tanger Med, and neither time did the authorities ask to see either the Pet Passport or the certificate, despite the fact they saw our dog so knew we had a pet. If you're unsure, consult your vet before leaving home or maybe a vet in Spain or Gibraltar.

Our King Charles Cavalier Spaniel in the Sahara at Erg Chebbi

Returning from Morocco

To return from Morocco into the EU, you need either a valid EU Pet Passport for each animal you're bringing back or an AHC issued by a vet in Morocco up to 10 days before travel. There is no need to visit a Moroccan vet for worming treatment.

If you use a Pet Passport it needs to be issued inside the EU. The UK Government website (*www.gov.uk/take-pet-abroad/overview*) states:

"You can enter or return to the UK with your pet cat, dog or ferret if it:

- has been microchipped
- has a pet passport or third-country official veterinary certificate
- has been vaccinated against rabies - it will also need a blood test if you're travelling from an 'unlisted country'"

As Morocco is an 'unlisted country', you will need a blood test to be carried out to prove the rabies vaccination was effective. The blood sample has to be taken at least 30 days after the vaccination. You'll also need to allow time for the results to come back (up to 15 working days) and for your vet to complete the Pet Passport or AHC, so plan ahead. If the vaccination blood test is failed, then you'll need to allow time for another one. Once again, we strongly recommend you discuss your plan to travel to Morocco with your vet as early as possible, so they can advise you on the latest legislation and provide any pet-specific guidance to you.

In our experience we have returned from Morocco to Spain twice with our King Charles Cavalier Spaniel, Charlie. The first time we handed over Charlie's Pet Passport to the Spanish customs authorities and they just handed it back. The second time the customs authorities looked through the passport then handed it back, without looking at Charlie or scanning his microchip. We worked on the assumption the authorities would carry out a full check of the document, including a microchip scan, and had everything in order just in case.

Other Pet Considerations

We also took the following actions in relation to our dog:

- Our dog's yearly booster vaccinations were up to date and would remain valid for the duration of the time we were in Morocco (a vet in Portugal carried out this task for us).
- We bought and fitted a Scalibor Collar to our dog while in Spain. The collar we chose provided protection against ticks, fleas and leishmaniasis for four to six months. Not all collars or other types of tick and flea treatment cover leishmaniasis, but it's endemic in Mediterranean regions and Morocco, so your pet should be protected against it. We have met people who found their dogs to be allergic to Scalibor collars, an alternative would be regular treatment with Advantix Spot On treatment.
- Our dog was prescribed Seraquin and Loxicom to help alleviate the impact of his arthritis. We assumed we couldn't get these in Morocco and arranged with our vet in the UK to have a year's supply of them with us.
- We had no pet insurance for Charlie, but if you have insurance it would be worth checking the policy wording or contacting the insurer to confirm what cover, if any, you would have in Morocco.
- We took a good supply of Charlie's dry dog food with us. We also needed to buy some in Morocco, which wasn't an issue for us as we don't always feed him the same brand of food. We found that supermarkets in the larger towns and cities stocked a small range of dog and cat foods, but if you need a consistent type of food, it would make sense to bring enough of it with you for your entire trip to Morocco.
- There is a lot of rubbish to on some of the streets of Morocco, if your dog is a scavenger like ours, be sure to keep it on a short lead. Charlie managed to snaffle something once that gave him a very upset stomach. Fortunately, we managed to treat him ourselves. We stayed on a campsite, so he didn't have to move and stopped feeding him for 24 hours. When we restarted it was with small amounts of plain pasta and water until he was able to keep his food in.

- Morocco stopped using plastic bags a few years back, so you can't source dog poop bags or nappy sacks. Depending on where we were we'd use a stick to flick any poop into a gutter or off the main footpath, or (ignoring the strange looks from locals) would use paper poop bags or as a last resort a plastic bag we brought with us, and dispose of it in a bin.
- When returning to the UK with a dog, you'll need to visit a vet abroad and have them treat your dog for tapeworms (Echinococcus Multilocularis) and update your AHC (or new EU Pet Passport).

Vets in Morocco

There are vets in Morocco. The ones we saw seemed to be generic, covering both farm animals and pets, and we only saw them in the larger towns and cities. Some Moroccans have pet dogs, even though they're considered a 'dirty' animal under Islam, requiring you to wash several times if a dog's saliva touches you or your clothing. As with any service in Morocco, if you find yourself in need of a vet, ask someone and they'll either know the local vet themselves, or know someone who does. If you're on a campsite, try the campsite owner or manager first.

If you struggle to find a local vet, the follow veterinary practices in large cities currently receive good reviews on Google, although they could be many hour's drive away. There are other vets available in these cities too should you need them – search for "Veterinaire Maroc" on Google to find them.

Marrakech - Clinique Vétérinaire Yasmine

www.cliniqueveterinaireyasmine.com
Open Mon to Fri from 9am to 1pm, then from 3pm to 7pm, and Sat 9am to 1pm
During business hours call: 00212 5244 58696
In emergencies out of hours, 24 hours, 7 days on these phone numbers: 00212 5244 58696 , 00212 5244 58697 or 00212 6617 29928
Address: Boulevard Prince Moulay Abdellah, Complexe Résidentiel Ben Tachefine
GPS: N31.6519005, W8.0179991

Casablanca – Cabinet Vétérinaire Californie
www.facebook.com/Cabinet-Vétérinaire-Californie-147910901919647
Open Mon to Fri from 9:30am to 4:30pm, Sat 9:30am to 2:30pm
Can be contacted by sending a Facebook Message via the above web address
Contact number: 00212 5228 73050
Address: Boulevard Fès, Lotissement Ghita, Lot 9, Californie, 20150 Casablanca
GPS: N33.544560, W7.614663

Entering Morocco: From Spain to Your First Night Stop

The process of entering Morocco is fairly simple but isn't entirely obvious at first. The following pages should help you smoothly enter Morocco at the start of your trip, and efficiently leave at the end.

Options for Ferries

There are numerous options for ferry routes from Spain, Italy, Gibraltar and France to Morocco, plus the option to travel to the Spanish enclaves of Ceuta and Melilla on the African continent, and drive over the border into Morocco.

Taking a ferry across the Strait of Gibraltar

For a list of ferry routes by all operators take a look at *www.directferries.com*. The shortest and most frequent crossings are

Algeciras to Tanger Med (60 to 90 minutes, with several companies completing up to eight crossings each per day) and Tarifa to the port in Tangier (60 minutes with two companies providing up to 8 crossings per day). The crossing times should be taken with a pinch of salt, as ferries are often late to board and once docked you can wait a good while before you're allowed off.

The directferries site also provides details for ferries from Algeciras to Ceuta, quoting crossing times of 70 minutes, and Almeria to Melilla, quoting a crossing time of 8 hours.

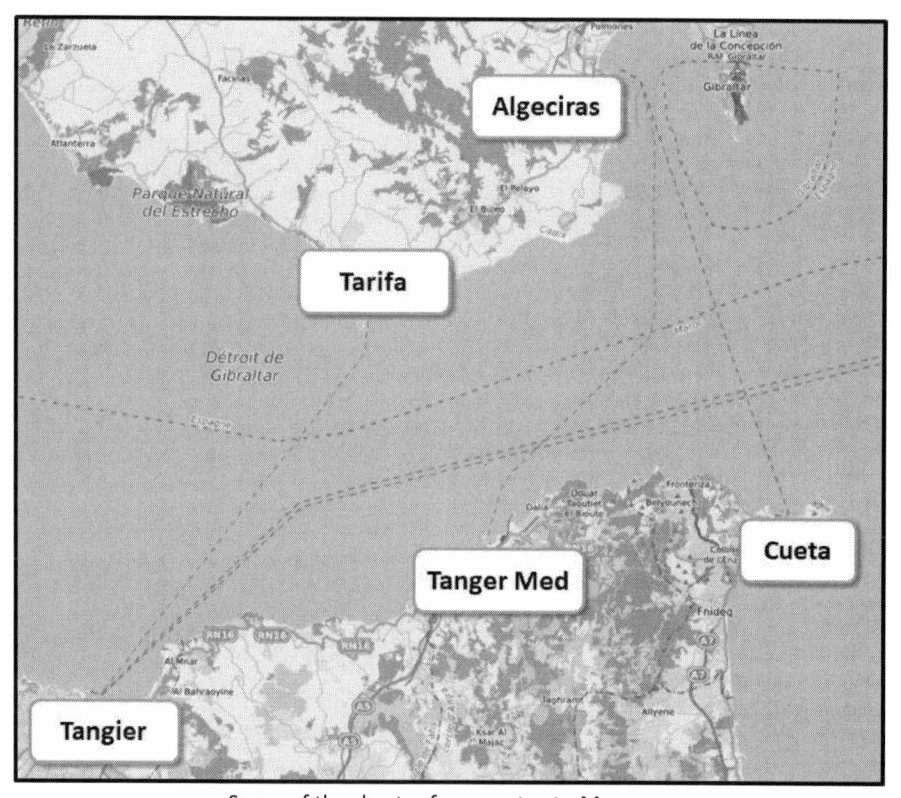

Some of the shorter ferry routes to Morocco

As we had a pet, and wanted to avoid the potentially busy land border at Ceuta, we opted for the shorter crossing route from Algeciras to Tanger Med. The first time we travelled we needed to buy third party insurance for our motorhome, and our research at the time showed only Tanger Med had an insurance office at the port. Our experience of using Tanger Med (which, despite the name, is an hour's drive from Tangier) has been good. Although the process of completing police and customs checks took a while and felt a little haphazard, it was nothing compared to our entry into Tunisia. The authorities are generally officious, but fairly friendly and not discourteous. There were no touts trying to make us pay for help to complete the entry process and no suggestion of bribes. The facilities were clean and new, and the access to the motorway network to head south is simple.

Buying Ferry Tickets

If you are travelling from or near to Algeciras, there is an established ticket sales office just off junction 112 of the N-340 which has a very good reputation for selling motorhome and caravan ferry tickets to Morocco – Viajes Normandie. This agency is so well known in the motorhome community it is often referred to by the founder's name, Carlos. The agency is open every day from 9am to 9pm.

>Viajes Normandie
>Calle Fragata 32
>11379 Los Barrios
>Cádiz
>
>info@viajesnormandie.com
>*viajesnormanie.net*
>Telephone: 0034 956 675 653
>GPS: N36.17916, W5.44111

The Viajes Normandie ferry ticket office

Viajes Normandie provide open ticket vouchers, valid for a year, so you don't need to know or book the specific ferry date and time you need. Under normal circumstances you just arrive at the Algeciras or Tanger Med port, and board the next available ferry back to Spain. The process for exchanging the voucher for a ticket is simple, see 'Catching the Ferry' section.

Vouchers for ferry tickets issued by Viajes Normandie

When buying your vouchers, note the following:

- The costs will vary with route and time of year, but as of 2020 prices from Algeciras to Tanger Med were around €200 (£170) return for a motorhome with two adults, or €220 (£190) return for a motorhome with two adults and a trailer. The ticket prices are the same regardless of the length of your motorhome.
- There was no extra cost for taking our dog with us, and he wasn't mentioned on the tickets. During the crossing he had to stay in the motorhome.
- Viajes Normandie speak mainly Spanish and French. If you speak neither, don't worry, as they've run through the ticket process so many times they'll be able to get the information from you that they need! You will be asked what route you want to take, what time you want to depart and if you have a *remorque*. This is French for a trailer. If you have one, tell them and they'll ensure your voucher covers it.
- Viajes Normandie only take cash, in Euros, they don't take cards. There is a cash machine around 50m away from the ticket office so make sure you have enough before you join the queue.

- You can obtain Moroccan Dirhams from official money changers in the port (or from the cash machines in most towns), but if you want to get some before arriving then Viajes Normandie will exchange some Euros for you.
- You need to take your passports and V5C with you when you buy the vouchers.

You will be given a pack containing your open vouchers for travel in each direction, immigration (white) and return (yellow) forms for each person travelling, and a few promotional leaflets for campsites. You used to be issued temporary vehicle import forms at this point (the D16 Ter forms) but these are now no longer needed – the customs in Morocco will print a temporary admission form for you. You'll also receive a complementary bottle of wine to raise a glass to your adventure, and maybe even a chocolate cake.

Top Tip: When booking your tickets, you'll be asked if you want the 8am or 10am ferry. If you know that you are not traveling far once you reach Morocco, ask for an early afternoon ferry as they will be less busy with motorhomes, making it quicker to get through customs.

Overnight Parking Before and After the Ferry

Viajes Normandie is on a retail estate surrounded by supermarkets, hardware stores, fast food restaurants, auto-factors and other outlets. There is plenty of parking on the estate, and for several years overnight parking for motorhomes has been tolerated. Viajes Normandie is in an office behind the Carrefour supermarket (GPS co-ordinates with contact details above).

Motorhomes currently park next to Mercadona supermarket (N36.183883, W5.437582). There are signs saying maximum weight 2.5t on the estate which are widely ignored. There were around 50 motorhomes there when we stopped, and the police passed by several times to check on us. There is also a motorhome aire (no services) closer to Viajes Normandie (N36.179194, W5.4391068), so there are several options for a free, quiet night's sleep before and after the ferry. The port is only 5km away along fast roads. The shops are also a great place to stock up before and after the voyage to and from Africa.

Informal motorhome parking in Algeciras near the ferry ticket agency

Stocking Up on Food and Alcohol – Remember Gibraltar

Morocco has enticing, cheap and authentic food. Tagines, couscous, chicken kebabs and various other delights await. A range of good quality olives, fresh fruit and vegetables, nuts, dates and dried figs are available everywhere, and for very little money. You may still wish to stock up on a few choice items before travelling to Africa though, to keep your variety of meals interesting, or to simply take items you love to eat.

Remember that Morocco is a Muslim country, so pork is generally not available as it's considered unclean under Islam. There's nothing to stop you taking in tinned, frozen or dried pork products. Alcohol is available in Morocco, but it's expensive, not always the best quality and not always easy to get. Note the points about import restrictions earlier in this book, and consider them before stocking up.

> One British couple we met were happily enjoying campsite life on the edge of the Sahara Desert in M'hamid. Checking their stash of beers, they discovered they had only a few left, so asked the campsite owner where they could get a few more. The answer: roughly two and a half hour's drive north at Zagora.

If you're from the UK, or enjoy some UK-specific foods, then Gibraltar is only a 30-minute drive from Algeciras. There is a secure motorhome aire on the Spanish side of the border at the marina at La Línea de la Concepción (N36.156372, W5.356651) for €12.50 (10.50) a night. From here you can walk to the border (don't forget to take your passport) and either shop at the Euroski supermarket just over the border, which stocks Waitrose products, or catch the bus, or walk fifteen minutes to Morrisons supermarket. Alternatively, you could drive into Gibraltar and park in Morrisons car park, but queues in and out of the enclave are sometimes long, the roads are narrow and even though the fuel is cheap, it's about the same price in Morocco.

Catching the Ferry

If you travel from Algeciras, the process to follow at the port is this:

1. Your vouchers list the times of the ferries, and you need to arrive an hour or so before your departure time to go through customs and board.
2. Drive to the port, following the signs to *Puerto (Norte)*. At the port, ignore anyone who claims you need to pay them anything extra to get your tickets, this is an old scam.
3. Drive to the entry lane with the logo of your ferry company above it and hand your voucher to the member of staff in the ticket booth and wait for your tickets to be returned to you.
4. Drive through passport control, showing your passports if requested, and then through customs, stopping if requested. During our crossings no-one was interested in the fact we had a pet on board.
5. Follow directions to the boarding area for your ferry and either start or join the queue for your ferry. Wait for your ferry to arrive and for any other vehicles to be loaded in front of you. When it's the turn of cars and motorhomes, someone will wave you on.

Note: turn off your gas using the isolator valves on top of the bottles before boarding, and if necessary switch your fridge to 12V to prevent it from trying to relight. Our fridge stayed cold for the duration of the crossing until we could relight it on gas again at Tanger Med port.

Ferry boarding (by reversing the lorries onto it) at Algeciras

6. Follow the directions of the staff. You may be required to drive down a ramp to a lower deck. Also, some ferries are not roll-on, roll-off, so you'll need to be prepared to reverse into position when boarding the ferry or reverse off the loading ramp at the other end. This can be nerve-wracking, but if you take your time, don't be rushed by anyone, and follow the waved instructions of the staff you should be OK.
7. If you're heading to Tanger Med or Tangier, you need to take your passports and white immigration forms with you when leaving your motorhome on the car deck. The next page describes what to do with them.

Passing through the Moroccan Border
This is the fun part, a first introduction to Africa!

Although the process feels haphazard, it invariably works as long as your documentation is in order, which it will be of course. We found the Moroccan border formalities varied a little between our entry in 2012 and our second entry in 2017 (and more frequent visitors have told us it tends to vary a little each time they visit), but the basic steps remain the same.

Approaching customs, entering Morocco at the Tanger Med port

We have only used the Tanger Med port. We chose Tanger Med partly to avoid the busier border crossing at Ceuta, partly because it has a direct A4 motorway connection, but mainly because there are no touts or 'helpers' like those we have heard about at Tangier port. If you take the ferry to Ceuta or Melilla you will be arriving in a Spanish enclave, so you will not go through this process until you drive to the Moroccan border. Procedures at Tangier, Cueta and Melilla borders may differ slightly but once again the basic steps will be the same; each member of your party needs to pass through Moroccan immigration control and customs, and you will need to temporarily import your motorhome into the country.

In terms of on-the-ground steps, this is the process to follow when entering Morocco via Tanger Med port:

1. When leaving your motorhome on the car deck, ensure you have your passports and white immigration forms with you (these will be in your pack from Viajes Normandie, or you'll find some either at the information desk on the ferry or with the immigration official. Complete one white immigration form (called a *fiche* in French, pronounced feesh) per person travelling. Write small, the area for writing isn't huge! The form is in French and Arabic and possibly English. If the form is not in English, these are the fields:

   Nom: last name
   Prénom: first name
   Nom de Jeune Fille: maiden name, if any
   Date et lieu de naissance: date and place of birth
   Nationalité: nationality
   Pays de residence habituelle: country of usual residence
   Profession: occupation
   N° de Passport/Date de deliverance: passport number and issue date
   Destination/provenance: going to and coming from (write in the Spanish town you're travelling from, and the town of the campsite for your first stop – Asilah for example)
   Adresse au Maroc: address in Morocco: write in the name of the first campsite you intend to visit
   Motif principal du voyage: main reason for travelling, just put a cross in the Tourisme box

2. On board the ferry, an official will install themselves somewhere on the boat and process your immigration forms. It'll be obvious where they are, as a queue will assemble. If you wait a while the queue will drop off and you'll likely have the official to yourself. Each person travelling will need to visit the official, handing over the completed white immigration form and their passport. The official will process them and hand back your passport with a stamp showing the date you're entering the country, and another stamp with an eight digit reference number. Check both stamps

are present, and that the number is clearly legible: you'll need it in order to complete the vehicle import forms.
3. When you disembark from the ferry, follow the *SORTIE* signs (or just follow the vehicle in front of you) to Moroccan customs (*douane* in French, pronounced doo-wann), which is in a covered area. Drive past the first set of booths, these are the police booths, and an official will indicate which lane you should join – if not, just join any lane which already has a vehicle in it. Park up where indicated, turn your engine off and consider turning your fridge on gas. The customs process can be quick, or it can take a couple of hours.
4. Wait in your vehicle. As the cars, vans and motorhomes in front of you are processed you'll be waved forwards. Drive your motorhome to where they indicate on the other side of the customs booths in a covered area.
5. A customs official will come to your vehicle and ask for your Carte Grise (your V5C) and your passports. Hand them over and wait until the official returns with your passports. This may take some time, and you may spot the same guy taking and returning documents to other vehicles in a seemingly random order, don't worry, he hasn't forgotten about you.
6. The paperwork for temporarily importing your motorhome has changed since 1 Jan 2019. You used to have to complete a D16 Ter form and give it customs. You no longer need to do this. Instead, customs will use your V5C to print off an Admission Temporaire (AT) form, and hand it back to you before you leave customs. When they give you the AT form, check carefully that the dates on it are correct (it should be valid for six months from the point of entry). Make sure you keep this form safe too: you'll need it when you come to leave Morocco.
7. If you have any other vehicles (a moped, quad bike and so on), then you'll need to get an AT form for them too. If any of the vehicles are not registered in your name, then the Moroccan customs website states you will need written proof of: "Power of attorney for the owner of the means of transport (case of importation of a vehicle belonging to a third party). The power of attorney is either duly legalized by the local authorities of the place of residence abroad of the owner of the car, or endorsed

by the Moroccan consulate in the country of residence." There is more information on the process here: www.douane.gov.ma (in French).

8. The official may wish to see inside your vehicle, ours did and carried out a very perfunctory search, opening a few cupboards and looking in the bathroom. Moroccans travelling back into the country seemed to be receiving far more thorough searches. When the official saw our dog he asked if we had the paperwork for him, we replied that we did, but he didn't ask to see any actual documents.

9. The customs official will then signal for you to drive out of the customs area. Just beyond, one final official will check your import documents have been completed before you leave the customs area.

10. There is a large parking area before you leave the port with a number of cabins providing currency exchange services, cash machines and telecoms shops selling mobile phone SIMs. We suggest obtaining some Dirhams here. The rates are advertised so you can walk along and compare them. We took €200 in cash with us to change so we didn't have to find a bank before our first stop. We also asked the money changer for some smaller notes and coins; ask for *petite monnaie* (small change in French, pronounced perteet monay). We also suggest not buying your SIM at this point, but instead to buy it later from a mainstream shop, so you can take your time choosing what you want, and ensure it is working before leaving the shop.

You can now leave the port and head for your first night's stopover. As you exit the port, you're taken onto the N16. If you opt to head south, after a mile or two you can turn onto the A4 motorway at a roundabout (only do this if you have Dirhams to pay for the tolls). Congratulations, you just drove into Africa!

First Night's Stop

Obviously, this book is about independent motorhome travel, and once you're in Morocco, you can go wherever you please! We've included a few suggestions for first night's stopover which we've used, are relatively close to Tanger Med port and are in towns which have Maroc Telecom shops in walking distance, so are handy if you want to buy an Internet SIM. If you arrive in Tanger Med late in the evening, other travellers report that you can stay safely in the port overnight.

Atlantic Coast - Asilah

If you plan to head south on the Atlantic coast Asilah is a pleasant town and the drive from Tanger Med port (60 – 90 minutes) can be done almost all on motorway. As of 2017, the A4 and A1 toll motorways to Asilah cost 71Dh in tolls (they only take Dirhams in cash) for a Class 2 vehicle, about £5.60. The campsites have basic facilities and are in walking distance of the town, and there also a guarded parking area right next to the medina (old town) walls, if you're feeling immediately brave.

The campsites are only around a mile or so from the motorway, and the roads to get through the town are relatively wide and quiet. We stayed at Camp As Saada (GPS: N35.471942, W6.02888). There is also a Maroc Telecom shop a couple of hundred metres towards the town – you should pass it on your right as you drive to the campsite from the motorway. The town's medina is well worth a visit, relaxed and easy going, a good introduction to Morocco and if you head out to town around sunset the restaurants and streets just outside the medina come to life.

Asilah, Atlantic Coast, Morocco

Mediterranean Coast – Martil

If you plan to head east, then Camping Al Boustane at Martil on the Mediterranean coast (GPS: N35.62890 W5.27736) is a good stop. The town isn't as pretty as Asilah, the site is fairly basic and the drive isn't quite as simple, heading north and east over the hills via the N16, then south on the A6 toll motorway, for which you will need Dirhams in cash (or you can stay on the N16). Martil is about three miles from the A6, and the campsite is in the town. There's a Maroc Telecom shop in the town, on Avenue Hassan II which is a short walk from the site.

The in-town campsite at Martil, Mediterranean Coast, Morocco

Inland and South East - Chefchaouen

The blue town of Chefchaouen in the Rif Mountains is about a 3 to 3.5 hour drive from Tanger Med. Despite the name, the Rif Mountains are more like rugged hills than the Alpine peaks you might imagine. Although the roads through them twist around, you won't be slogging your way up one in four inclines in first gear to get to Chefchaouen. The town is very pretty, welcoming and there is a weekly souk on a Thursday, which is a sight to see if you've never seen one before. To get there you can start off on the A4 motorway (in 2017, 28Dh for a Class 2 vehicle, about £2.20), but then you need to turn off and onto the N2, which is not as easy to drive as the motorway. The road is tarmacked, but is winding and narrow in places, passing through towns and villages that can be fairly busy with traffic.

The Chefchaouen townscape

This being the Rif Mountains, you may well find people trying to sell you drugs, in particular marijuana. From our experience, and anecdotal evidence from others, the dealers are a friendly lot, but being pulled over by a dealer in a 4x4 offering you *chocolate* or *kif* might not be what you fancy on Day 1. By the time you leave Morocco this will all be a piece of cake, but for a first day's drive, there are easier places to stay.

The medina at Chefchaouen is painted in shades of blue

The Chefchaouen Camping Azilan is on a hill to the west of the old town (GPS: N35.175603, W5.267009) and is easy to access in a motorhome. The campsite takes tents as well as motorhomes, and the parking area is flat and gravelled. The showers and toilet block are usable, but aren't well maintained so we used the facilities in our van. If you want to brave the campsite showers we were advised that the first door on the right, which is often bolted on the outside, is the only hot one. You can walk down to the blue medina on a path which runs past the Hotel Atlas and down through the graveyard (best to take the long way around on a Friday to avoid offending locals).

> When we visited in 2017, the site seemed to have acquired a pet donkey, who roamed between the vans begging for food! After feeding it a banana, we quickly regretted it when it took not one, but two enormous pees on our plastic rug, which stunk afterwards despite being washed.

West – Tangier

If you're heading west, you may want to visit the old town of Tangier. Camping Miramonte is on the western edge of the town, about a twenty minute walk to the medina (GPS: N35.79086, W5.83101). Tangier is about an hour's drive from Tanger Med, down the A4 toll motorway before heading north-west on the N2. The drive is more difficult than Asilah, and the last time we visited, confusingly we had to drive into the port and around the northern edge of the town, facing the coast, to reach the campsite.

The campsite is on a steep hill, which was easy to pass in a 5.5m long motorhome but vehicles over 7m might struggle. The site facilities are of a poor quality but the site feels safe and is the only place available to park overnight in Tangier. There are several Maroc Telecom shops in Tangier; the one closest to the campsite is on Avenue Imam Mouslim (N35.785163, W5.824835).

Extending Your 3 Month Visa

You can stay up to 6 months in a calendar year in Morocco without applying for citizenship. However, visitors are only issued with a 3 month visa on entry to the country. If you want to stay longer than 3 months, you have two options:

- Leave Morocco and re-enter, by driving into one of the Spanish enclaves, Ceuta or Melilla, or by taking a ferry back to Spain for a day or two and returning.
- Extend your visa by going through an official process.

Although we haven't extended our visas, we've met people who have, and have also read in various guidebooks and forums how straightforward it is. Some campsites will go through the process for you, and we saw adverts for this at receptions of several campsites, especially those in south on the Atlantic coast. The overall cost seems to be fairly low – maybe only £20 for two people.

The exact steps to follow vary between provinces in Morocco, but in all cases you will need to submit multiple copies of various documents: the ID page in your passports, the page in your passport with the Moroccan number stamp, handwritten application letters, certificates of stay from your campsite, your credit card details, and several passport photos. If you are thinking of extending your visa, we were told that it is worth having a set of passport photos taken before you travel to Morocco. For more information, search Google for *'prolongation sejour maroc'* and use Google Translate to render the results into English.

Leaving Your Vehicle in Morocco

If you need to fly home during your stay we understand you can place your vehicle into customs protection while you're away (as long as the vehicle isn't in Morocco for more than 6 months a year). We've never been through this process and know of no-one who has, but if you find you need to do it, it would make sense to talk to your campsite reception about it as soon as you know you need to do it, or find your nearest customs office.

Leaving Morocco: Returning to Spain

When your tour is over, you'll be pleased to hear that the process of leaving Morocco at Tanger Med is simpler than the process of entering! These are the steps to follow, which again may be slightly different when you cross:

1. Complete a yellow immigration exit form for each person travelling. These are almost the same as the white entry forms you completed when entering Morocco.
2. Drive to the Tanger Med port, either along the great quality but toll A4 motorway, or the slower, more winding but free N16.

Top Tip: mobile speed cameras were in operation on the approach to the port, keep to the limit.

3. Just before the port you might find a few guys in high-vis jackets frantically waving at you to stop at their ticket shops. They're selling ferry tickets, and if you have an open return, you won't want any. Just raise a hand in thanks, touch your heart with the same hand and smile, and they'll leave you alone.
4. Follow the automobile access signs to a large parking area in front of a set of covered cabins/ticket offices. Park up and walk over to the cabins with your ticket vouchers. You may want to pop your fridge on gas now as you may be a while in the queue.
5. Find the cabin for your ferry company, queue up and hand them your ticket vouchers. Some companies will only let you check in a couple of hours before the next ferry is due. The cabin assistant will check you in for the next available ferry. They may ask again if you have a trailer (*remorque*) and will then issue you tickets for the ferry. We checked in at 4.30pm, so our tickets were for the 7pm ferry, however we knew that the 4pm ferry was running late (we had friends waiting for it) so we went through customs, joined the queue with them and caught the earlier ferry, which didn't actually leave until 6pm!
6. The area that you changed money in on arrival is just behind the check-in cabins, so you can swap any remaining Dirhams for Euros.

7. Once you are checked in, drive between the check in cabins and money change area, here an official will check your tickets and point at the lane to get into. Drive along the lane until you reach the police booths. Stop here and hand the policeman the yellow exit forms and your passports. Wait for the passports to be returned then drive on.
8. Stop at the customs (*douane*) booths and hand them your AT vehicle import form. Wait for them to process the forms and wave you on, then drive to the queue for the X-ray machine. We kid you not.
9. All vehicles have to X-rayed and this is done by a machine mounted onto a truck which drives along a raised platform and scans the vehicles. Follow the instructions and drive onto the raised platform (you'll be called forward to the stopping point if you're the first on). Once parked on it, switch off your engine and all people and animals need to leave the vehicle and wait under the adjacent covered area.
10. Once the X-ray truck has driven past all the vehicles, you can return to your motorhome and drive it around to the covered area. Turn the engine off and wait for a customs official to either come and look in your vehicle (the first time we did this we had to show the leisure battery, but not the second), or to wave you on.
11. Drive on, following the signs to the quayside and then look for the queue for your ferry. The names of the ferry company and departure times are on signs. If you miss it, you can turn round and look for it again. Once you've found it, join the back of the queue and wait. Before loading an official will come and take your tickets and leave part of them under your windscreen wiper.
12. You may want to leave your fridge on gas for now, as it could take some time for the ferry to arrive, dock and unload. However, don't forget to turn off your gas at the bottles when loading of vehicles in your queue starts, and switch the fridge to 12V. There is a duty free shopping area on the quayside if you have any Dirhams left, or you just want to pass some time.
13. During loading, follow the instructions of the staff in high vis. Again you may need to reverse while on the ferry in order to ensure you can drive off it at the Spanish side.

14. Once on the ferry there is nothing to do but relax, and maybe have a bite to eat. The duty free shop and restaurant on our ferry only took Euros or cards, so make sure you have some with you if you want to buy anything. You could also stand on deck and look for wildlife, we spotted a few pods of pilot whales on our first trip over the Strait of Gibraltar.
15. When you've docked in Spain, wait for an instruction to return to your vehicle. Once given the go-ahead, drive off the ferry and follow instructions through police and customs controls, handing over your passports and pet passports as requested.
16. Once through the formalities at the border, obviously you can drive wherever you like. As it was dark by the time we docked, we opted to return to the informal motorhome parking area close to the Viajes Normandie ticket agent (see above), where we stayed for two nights and restocked with food and drinks.

Note: the Moroccan customs website (*www.douane.gov.ma*) indicates that foreigners leaving Morocco can take the following items out of the country (with suitable proof of payment) without having to go through customs formalities. If you buy any antiquities or other such items, be aware you may not be able to export them.

"Products of Moroccan origin (crafts or other) acquired locally and this, without limitation of value. The justification of the settlement is made by any appropriate means (exchange slip, international credit card, traveller's cheque, etc.). Travel souvenirs: Ornamental, fossiliferous and / or semi-precious stones (provided that they do not exceed ten)"

Driving in Morocco

We joke that driving in Morocco is like a hazard perception test. There are so many sights to see, many of which are walking down the road, that you need to concentrate and not expect to get anywhere fast. Moroccan drivers seem to have acquired a legendary status as crazed maniacs, but that's not true. As with everywhere you'll find lots of careful drivers, but also some drivers who aren't paying attention and some who are carrying loads no-one in their right mind would try and carry in Europe. Read on for some advice gleaned from our time driving around the country, as well as anecdotes from fellow travellers.

Where else but Morocco can you see this as you drive?

The Basics – Drive on the Right!

OK, first up the absolute basics of driving in Morocco:

- Drive on the right. You may occasionally be surprised to see someone driving the wrong way around a roundabout or down a dual carriageway on your side of the road. Yep, a few Moroccans will do that, but only for a short distance to save them from driving the long way round, they don't do it for miles on end, usually!

- Drive in daylight. Avoid driving at night as you'll be needing as much light as you can get to spot the potholes, donkeys, people, goats, carts and mopeds in the road.
- Speed limits are posted with standard speed limit signs and are in kilometres. They are generally 60KPH in towns, 100KPH outside urban areas and 120KPH on the motorways. The Moroccan police are hot on catching speeding motorists, so pay close attention, especially in 60 KPH areas as we saw many mobile speed camera units pulling lots of drivers over, including us! We found it best to assume that once you pass the sign for a town, the speed limit is 60 until you reach the other side or see a sign saying otherwise (in some towns it goes down to 40 KPH).
- According to the World Health Organisation (*apps.who.int*), the maximum blood alcohol concentration limit in Morocco is 0.02% (it's 0.08% in England). If you're caught over the limit, the fines range from 5000 to 10000 Dirhams, or up to 6 months in prison.
- The road signs are pretty much the same as those you'll see in Europe with distances in kilometres. They're usually in both Arabic script and in Roman script, so you'll have a chance at spotting the letters CASABLANCA alongside الدار البيضاء! Some STOP signs are only in Arabic, but are always in a red octagon like at home, and look like this:

A STOP sign in Arabic

Navigation

We've already discussed maps and GPS systems in the 'Preparation before you go' section, so now we will look at navigation and planning for your daily drives.

Note: The 969-mile-long land border between Morocco and Algeria has been closed since 1994 after a dispute over a terrorist attack in Marrakech, and shows no sign of being re-opened. You cannot legally drive between the two countries.

All of Morocco is in the northern hemisphere, and west of the Greenwich Meridian. This means you either need to enter N and W into your GPS system, or use a positive number for north, and a negative number for west. When planning a route or navigating you will notice inconsistencies in the spelling of Moroccan place names on maps, signs, GPS systems, books and websites. For example, Marrakech is also spelt Marrakesh, or Fes as Fez, the reason for this is explained later in the 'Day to Day basics' section.

While the speed limits in Morocco are generally 60KPH in towns, 100KPH outside urban areas and 120KPH on the motorways, much of the time you'll not be able to get up to these speeds. Winding roads through mountains, slow lorries, poor surface conditions, narrow sections of road, chaotic market day conditions in towns, the scenery, police road blocks, animals in the road and the fact you become tired from constant attention will all conspire to make your journeys last longer than you'd expect. We looked at our map and the distance we would be travelling, looked at the time guessed by maps.me, and added a third. That seemed to work as a very rough rule of thumb.

The Moroccan road network is constantly improving and paper maps cannot keep up, this is where a regularly updated GPS or satnav will come into its own. While staying in the guarded parking under palms in the oasis of Aït Mansour, the guardian Mustapha took our map and drew a road on where none existed before. The road ran from the southern end of the gorge west towards Azerbi, and meant we could drive through the spectacular mountain oasis, and through no-less impressive landscapes of the arid Anti-Atlas Mountains, an unforgettable drive on what we now call the 'biro road'.

Driving down the 'Biro' road

Top Tip: Don't rely on your satnav or GPS system. Satnavs like to please you by taking you the shortest or fastest route to your destination. Please don't follow the instructions blindly, always double-check against a map as not all 'satnav shortcuts', as we like to call them, are suitable for motorhomes, as our friends found out.

> In 2017 we spent some of the time in Morocco travelling with friends. A couple of days after entering the country we travelled ahead of them on a route from Asilah to Ouezzane. Maps.me suggested we turn east off the N1 onto the P4208 near to Arbaoua. We slowed down at the junction, took a look at the rapidly-thinning tarmac on the small road heading east, checked our map and opted to take the longer route, staying on the main road.
>
> When we met our friends at the campsite outside Ouezzane that evening, they were frazzled. Having followed their GPS's advice they turned onto the P4208 only to have it go from bad to worse. With not enough tarmac to have all four wheels on the road at the same time, in places there were drop offs a foot high on each side of the road. They managed to not inflict any damage to their motorhome, and had a few fun encounters with locals along the way, but it was hard going. On the Michelin map the road shows as a *piste* (described later on), which are usually best avoided if there's a better road.

Road Types and Surface Conditions

The following section runs through the types of road you'll find in Morocco. The road categorisations are those used on the Michelin 742 National map, and we've given our view of the state of those road types from the point of view of driving a two-wheel drive motorhome on them.

The Michelin National 742 map seems to be the best available paper map, but as mentioned above it's perpetually out of date. The Moroccan road network is being upgraded all of the time, and roads which show as unsurfaced piste roads on the map may well have been surfaced by the time you arrive. Conversely, what looks like a good road on the map may have long sections of road works (in places miles long) where you have to drive on dirt roads. Asking campsite owners, fellow travellers or using online forums seems to be the best way to get an idea of the latest road conditions.

Motorways (Autoroutes, A Roads)

Morocco has around 1100 miles of fast, quiet and good quality motorways running north-south (from Tanger Med port to Agadir, via Marrakech) and east-west (from Casablanca to Beni Mellal and from Rabat to Oujda by the border with Algeria, via Fes). The motorway network has a general speed limit of 120 KPH (about 74 MPH). These are toll roads, administered by Autoroutes du Maroc (ADM - *www.adm.co.ma*). You pay the tolls in cash, Dirhams only, at booths along the way. You can also see a real-time traffic and roadworks status of these motorways, and even webcams via ADM's website. If you have a smartphone, have a look at the Ma Route app, which gives similar real-time road information.

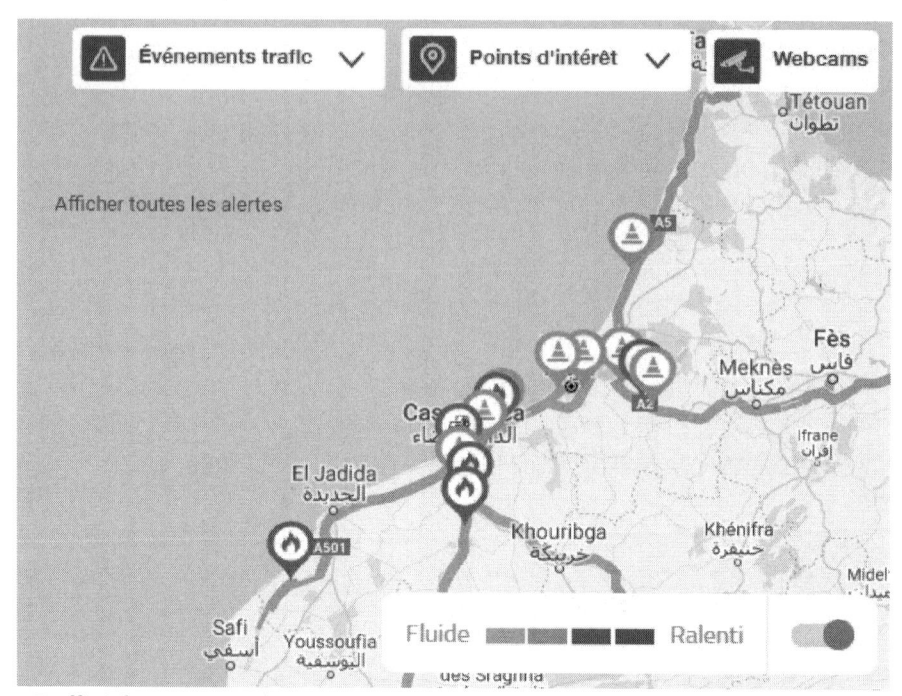

Traffic information on the Autoroutes du Maroc website (ADM - *www.admtrafic.ma*)

Three vehicle classifications are used to determine prices. Motorhomes will be either Class 2 (vehicles with 2 axles greater than 1 m 30) or Class 3 (vehicles or assemblies with more than 2 axles greater than 1 m 30) if you're towing a high trailer for example.

As a very rough idea of toll (*péage*, pronounced pay-arj) costs, a Class 2 vehicle from Tanger Med to Asilah in 2017 was 71Dh, and a Class 3 was 86Dh. From Asilah to Kenitra was 82Dh and 99Dh for Class 2 and 3 respectively. As you approach the motorway you will see a sign with the toll prices on it, there are also signs on the toll booth ticket machines. The price shown is from the junction you are at, so just look for the junction you are going to get off at and your vehicle class to work out the price.

Note: We've heard from fellow travellers who've used the motorway services (*aires de service*) for overnight stays without issues but have no direct experience of doing this ourselves.

Motorway toll ticket collection – head for the lane with the green arrow. You hand the ticket over at a later set of booths and pay the amount they ask for.

Major Roads – Shown in Red

Major roads join up the towns across Morocco. If you wish, you can avoid motorway tolls and mundaneness by taking the red routes which shadow them. Where motorways don't exist, red roads are usually the fastest way around, and are generally good quality. The surfaces are tarmacked, but in places you'll find the surface uneven and the roads narrow. Coupled with the various hazards you will comes across (see below), speeds on these roads are likely to be fairly slow, averaging maybe only 40 MPH.

Red roads can be busy in some places with lorries, tourist coaches, taxis and a whole host of other types of vehicles, so secondary routes are sometimes a better option.

In some places the major roads spread into wide and fast dual carriageways. We found this when travelling from Marrakech to Essaouira. About half way through the journey the road switched to four lanes of smooth tarmac, with no tolls, and we cruised along at a good speed. Conversely in very remote places (like the N12 east of Icht) they can switch to single-lane, requiring you to slow down and put two wheels on adjacent gravel when passing oncoming traffic.

The major route to Essaouira. Even fast roads sometimes have slow-moving traffic!

Major roads will almost always run through each of the towns along the route, not bypassing them. This both slows you down and offers you the option to either take a look at the place while you drive through, or pull up and go shopping. Outside of towns these roads have few lay-bys, and on the more popular tourist routes each lay-by that does exist seems to be 'owned' by a local or two. As you pull up to take a break or grab a photo, don't be surprised to get a knock at the door or a smiling face at the window, offering you the opportunity to buy whatever they have to offer!

> While staying at the Zebra Camp near the Cascade d'Ouzoud, the owners of the site expressed surprise when we asked whether we could take a shortcut back to the N8 to the north, so we could travel more quickly down to Marrakech. "Yes, the road north is sealed and a good road, but why would you want to use the N8, it's an awful road, full of traffic and no scenery? Take the yellow roads instead (the R304 and R210)." They were right, the secondary roads were quiet, good quality and had a great view of the High Atlas Mountains to the south.

Secondary Road – Shown in Yellow

Secondary roads tend to again be good quality tarmac, are usually two lanes, and are easily suitable for motorhomes. In our experience they were generally quieter than the major roads, but were slower as they tended to be less direct.

A secondary road in the Rif Mountains

Surfaced Roads – White with Solid Lines

Surfaced roads offer a great opportunity to get off the beaten path. They're sealed with tarmac, although in places they may only be a single track. Even then you should be able to have all of your wheels on the road unless you're pulling in to let someone overtake or getting out of the way of an oncoming vehicle. These roads can change between tarmac and piste in between towns, so if you're not sure about a particular route, take local advice before starting your journey.

White roads are surfaced, but can be narrow with some rough sections like this

In very rural areas, roads can appear, or disappear out of nowhere

Pistes – White with One side Dashed

Unsurfaced roads are called *pistes* in Morocco (pronounced peests), and are made up of packed rock and earth, but can also be very rough or deep sand. Some are passable in a standard two-wheel drive motorhome, driving slowly (maybe only 15KPH) and carefully. Some campsites are reached by sections of piste between a few hundred meters and several kilometres long. In general, unless you have a specialised off-road vehicle or are just using a piste to pass roadworks, do your research before taking piste roads. You could easily find yourself stuck or damage your tyres or suspension on rougher tracks, or just find yourself frazzled after miles on end of rough road.

A piste road north of Icht which we accidentally took...

Mountain Passes

Looking at Morocco from Spain, you can already see the mountainous nature of the country. The main mountain chains are the Rif in the north, the Middle and High Atlas running south-west to north-east, and the Anti-Atlas in the south. They all offer some spectacular scenery, in particular the High and Anti-Atlas. Sticking to the red major roads, the passes over these mountains are straightforward, two lanes of good quality tarmac with crash barriers and even crawler lanes in places. There aren't too many hairpins on the major roads, and those that exist are broad and easy to navigate, at least in a 6 to 7m long motorhome.

Mountain passes in Morocco can be snow-covered in winter. Snow gates (*Barrière de Neige*) are used to prevent travel onto snow-covered roads, and snow ploughs keep main routes open. It pays to keep an eye on the weather forecast and take local advice to avoid getting stuck at a gate. We found ourselves unable to move from a campsite at only about 850m above sea level, near the dam at Bin-el-Ouidane in the Middle Atlas in January. Snow fell on the passes either side of us, closing the road for a day or so.

The easiest high pass (*col* in French, *tizi-n* in Arabic) over the High Atlas Mountains in the north is the N13 between Midelt and Ar Rachidia. The mountains are fairly low at this point, and while the Ziz Gorge offers some great scenery, you'll hardly notice you're crossing a mountain range. For a real impression of the High Atlas, the Tizi–n-Tichka pass between Ouarzazate and Marrakech tops out at 2260m. Built by the French military in 1936, the modern route is very impressive but is a good quality, wide paved road.

The Tizi-n-Tichka Mountain Pass

The Anti-Atlas Mountains offer a very different landscape to the High Atlas but are no less impressive in terms of their outlandish rocks and lush oases. The road from Tiznit up to the Col du Kerdous is impressive and was easily passable in our 3.5 tonne motorhome. Numerous other less well-travelled routes through these mountains are just as incredible. We took the road south from Izerbi to the small mountain oasis at Igmir, which was jaw-dropping (just don't travel on any further south after Igmir as the road turns to very rough piste for many kilometres). Friends took the Tizi-n-Ounzour north of Tisnassemine (itself north of Tata) and found it equally rewarding.

Getting Around

Driving in Morocco is certainly more difficult than in most of Europe, but we've done it, so anyone can. The key to safe and enjoyable journeys is time. Unless you're just ploughing along the motorway, allow plenty of time for even short journeys. You're certain to come across all kinds of hazard which might not be familiar to first time travellers in Morocco, and you'll find yourself staring from the windows at incredible sights as you drive. We found trying to keep non-motorway journeys down to relatively short hops of three hours worked well for us, although we might only be able to travel 40 or 50KM in an hour. For an idea of some of the distractions and hazards you'll come across, read on.

Market Days in Towns

Moroccan towns have retained the tradition of a weekly (sometimes twice a week) market day, or souks. You'll know if you're approaching a town on souk day, as every man and his donkey will have arrived and will be swarming about the pavements and, more often than not, the road itself.

Market day means driving mayhem in Morocco!

The sight is intoxicating, and it is worth trying to find somewhere to park (good luck) and have a look around as the souks are a great experience. When driving through a town, particularly on souk day, take it very steady. Some pedestrians appear to have zero awareness of the fact they're stepping or pushing their bike into the road. Cars and vans will reverse out, pull up alongside the road or just crawl along looking for somewhere to park.

Pedestrians, Donkeys, Traps, Lorries, Bikes and Taxis

Moroccan roads reflect the huge range in wealth and technological advancement seen across the country. On the roads you'll pass everything from ladies and/or donkeys walking for miles hauling loads of sticks or plants on their backs, while 4x4s zoom past them, to hugely overloaded lorries with a driver peering through a gap in the stickers adorning the windscreen.

Lorries carry a bit more than they normally would in Europe.

Taxis in particular are worth keeping a close eye on while driving. They can be split into two types, 'Petits Taxis' which operate within a town or city boundary and 'Grands Taxis' which ply the routes between towns and cities. They range in age from ancient Mercedes to shining new Dacias, but regardless of age or mechanical condition, they like to make progress through the traffic. The Grands Taxis carry up to six passengers, and frequently stop with little or no notice to drop someone off or pick someone up at the side of the road.

You name it, you'll see it on the road in Morocco

Hitchhikers

You'll soon become accustomed to seeing people waiting at the side of the road for a Grand Taxi or a lift. Few vehicles travel without a full complement of passengers, and you may get the feeling that empty space in your motorhome is in high demand. Those wanting a lift will raise a hand, point up the road or wave it up and down in a 'slow down' motion. We've only given lifts a handful of times, partly as our dog has freaked out a few potential hitchhikers in the past, but we spoke with fellow British motorhome travellers who made it a point to pick up locals. On two occasions they helped locals get to hospital, and had nothing but good experiences. Our friends also gave a couple of schoolchildren a lift, disappointed to find themselves being begged from when they dropped the children off.

Another couple relayed to us how they fell for the almost infamous scammer who pretends his car has broken down on the N9 heading south into the Drâa Valley, finding themselves unable to be rid of him as he took them to various shops and restaurants many miles along the route (see 'Confusions and Annoyances' section). While giving a lift to those in need is part of the culture in Morocco, and a great way to help out the locals and get spend time with them, sadly it has been spoiled by a few trying to take advantage. The decision whether to pick up hitchhikers or not is entirely up to you.

Roadworks

You can find yourself driving along a perfectly good, sealed road, when a series of rapidly decreasing speed limit signs appears in front of you: 60, 40, 20. Then you find yourself being either directed off the road onto a dirt road running parallel with the sealed one, or discover that the surface of the road you're on has been ripped up. The diversions might be due to the road being resurfaced, or due to damage caused by the weather (see below), or some other improvements. The diversions we came across were always passable, but some routes would have set after set of roadworks, which would involve miles of piste road. Don't assume that a road is good just because it shows as sealed on the map, you might end up taking twice as long to rumble your way to your destination.

Like in the rest of the World, sometimes there are road work speed limit signs with no road works...

Fords and Bridges

The more arid areas of Morocco are criss-crossed by river beds (*oueds*, pronounced ooo-eds) which are dry almost all of the time. Roads cross these oueds using concrete fords or low bridges, not much more than pipes covered in concrete. Heavy rain falls from time to time, rushing off mountains and hills, flash-flooding river beds and flooding the fords. Obviously, this makes the fords impassable during the floods, but even in dry weather the road surface at fords is often roughed up by the boulders forced over them by the flood waters. As you're driving, you can spot fords in the distance from signs, or the small, flat-topped concrete pyramids placed along the side of the road. Some roads have ford after ford after ford.

Fords are almost always dry in Morocco

Note: the police advised us that all bridges in Morocco (which we assume meant all those except those on motorways), are treated as accident blackspots with a 60KPH speed limit. Even if the speed reduction isn't posted on signs, they advised us the limit applies for a short distance before and after the bridge too.

Police Road Blocks or Checkpoints

Police routinely slow down or stop traffic in order to carry out checks on the drivers and their vehicles. The stops are normally at the entrance or exit of a town, but can be anywhere. They look a little intimidating at first, stone-faced uniformed and armed men stand alongside or in the road, with tyre-flattening stinger devices ready to be pulled across the road. In practice, as a motorhome tourist you're very unlikely to be stopped. We've passed dozens of these checkpoints, and were waved through every time. There was never any suggestion of any kind of payment or bribe being needed to pass these checkpoints by foreign tourists, but we always smiled and waved thanks to the officers.

There are two types of checkpoint: the first is marked with a SLOW or *RALENTIR* sign. For these you only have to slow down to about 20KPH, and drive through looking at the police to show them you could stop if you had to. The second is marked STOP or *HALTE*, and they mean it. You have to stop at the sign, and wait for the police to wave you forwards. The policemen's waves are sometimes a bit hard to spot, as they don't usually lift their arm and do a full wave.

Note: If you plan to travel to the Western Sahara region of Morocco to the far south, checkpoints there are more rigorously applied to motorhomes, requiring *fiches* (similar to those completed on the ferry) to be completed at each stop. It may be worth having pre-prepared details to hand based on the immigration form in the 'Entering Morocco' section. The administration of this region has been in international dispute since the Spanish left in 1975. A war followed until 1991 when the UN sponsored a ceasefire. From a Moroccan perspective, Western Sahara is Moroccan, and the subject remains a taboo. Although violence appears to have been long over, we opted not to travel to Western Sahara mainly because it's a huge distance to travel, and there's enough desert in Morocco without travelling to this region. If you do opt to head south of Tan-Tan, it would make sense to check on the latest status of the region first.

Police Speed Traps

While motorhome tourists get away without being stopped at police checkpoints, speed traps are another matter. You're likely to pass quite a few mobile radar guns on your travels, and if you're more than 10% over the speed limit (66KPH in a 60KPH area) then you'll be stopped. If you are stopped, turn your engine off and be prepared to hand over the driver's driving license (photocard part only), your V5C, passport and copies of your vehicle import documents. The speed traps we saw were all in 60KPH areas on the edge of or between towns.

A mobile police radar trap in Morocco

> We were stopped for speeding at the exit of the motorway at Beni Mellal, after the toll booths where the road bends to rejoin the major road network. The policeman showed us a photo of our van on his radar gun indicating we were travelling at 68KPH after passing a 60KPH sign –a fair cop. We were asked to produce our documents, which were taken to the police car along with 150Dh in cash to pay the fine (about £12). Another driver was stopped and his fine was 300Dh, double the price of ours because he was driving at double the speed limit! After about 15 minutes our documents were returned with a detailed receipt, and we were cheerfully waved on our way. We met several other motorhomers who were also stopped for speeding.

Weather

The weather can make driving conditions difficult in Morocco. Wind can be an issue in desert areas, creating dust storms. We've only experienced this once in M'hamid, and fortunately it wasn't particularly bad, but still we opted not to drive in it to avoid risking clogging our air filter. Camped alongside the sand dunes at Erg Chebbi we also experienced small twisters, nothing major but enough to lift a neighbour's carpet 10m into the air.

Heavy rain causes flash floods most winters which can close roads for several hours. Keep an eye on the weather forecast and if heavy rain is predicted you may want to head for a campsite with a tarmac road and stable pitches which is away from a river bed for a couple of days (some sites in Sidi Ifni are by the river, and were entirely washed away in 2014 only to be rebuilt in the same locations).

Washed away bridge after heavy rain

On the night of 21 Feb 2017 we were in Camping de la Vallée near Abaynou (GPS: N29.11414, W10.019896) when very heavy rain woke us up. Thinking nothing of it, we eventually got back to sleep. The next morning we were stunned to find the dry river bed at the campsite entrance was now a torrent, and a motorhome which had tried to cross the ford was stranded in the water.

The elderly owners of the motorhome had attempted to cross before the water got too high, but in doing so caused the piste road to collapse. They had to be rescued by the site warden with a rope because the lady was unable to swim, and had water up to her chest. They were fine and the following the day the site population came together to push and pull the motorhome free, although it suffered water damage inside.

The site owner arranged for a JCB to remake the road, which was washed away in three places, allowing us to leave a day later. It pays to respect the weather in Morocco, and ask for advice from site owners where possible if you're unsure about what you plan to do.

Take care driving in wet conditions in Morocco

Dealing with a Breakdown

As we were driving through the stupendous landscapes of the Anti-Atlas or the roads edging the sub-Sahara, the thought of breaking down in such a remote place was enough to get us sweating, regardless of the heat!

On our second trip to Morocco we got chatting with the owners of Zebra Camp in Ouzoud. These were old hands at Africa, a Dutch couple who sold their business in the Netherlands, bought an old 4x4 and spent four years touring Africa, before setting up the campsite. When we asked them about breaking down, and how to handle it, they laughed, and we suspect this is a question they've had many times. "It is simple, don't worry" he said, "just flag someone down. Tell them you need a *mécanique* or if you know you need recovery to a garage, ask for a *dépannage*" and someone will ALWAYS come". "I once broke down deep in the desert and a breakdown truck came to recover me, it's no problem, you just need to allow time".

He went on to explain a 4x4 staying on the campsite needed a new part. A *mécanique* arrived after a few hours, looked at the vehicle and declared he'd go and get the part. When the owner of the 4x4 became impatient the campsite owner explained that the mechanic would call his friend in the next city, and tell him which part was needed. His friend would find the part and dispatch it with someone in a taxi coming back to where it was needed. The process would take a day or two, not an hour or two like back home.

On the final day of our three-month tour of Morocco, as we were driving to the port, we hit a pothole in some roadworks, and our van's engine died and wouldn't restart. Mild panic set in, and after a fruitless rummage in the engine bay, we were stuck.

While one of us asked for help online from the Hymer Owners Group Facebook group, the other stood by the roadside and looked miserable. The second vehicle passing stopped and asked if we needed help. Two young Moroccan guys, neither of whom spoke any English or French, managed to understand the problem, called someone who spoke English and arranged for a mechanic to get to us after Friday prayers. In the meantime, several responses had come back from the Facebook group, explaining there was a safety cut-off fuel switch which needed resetting. We found it, pushed the button and were on our way, having profusely thanked our Moroccan helpers, who had stayed with us for over an hour, made many phone calls, and yet asked for nothing in return.

In the Event of an Accident

Apart from clipping wing mirrors with a lorry, which resulted in no damage, we didn't have any accidents while driving in Morocco. While researching this book, we were unable to find one consolidated source for what to do if you're involved in an accident in your motorhome, especially if anyone has been hurt, so we've collated the below from various forums and websites:

- The official contact numbers for the police is 19 in cities and 177 for the Gendarmerie Royale outside of cities, or 15 for fire and medical services. However these numbers only work from a Moroccan phone and may only be of use if you speak good Arabic, Berber or French. If you are involved in an accident in a town or city, it seems more sensible to just look for the police or ask someone to get them for you.
- Contact your insurer and explain to them what has happened. Make sure you have a pen and paper available so you can make a note of any advice they give you.
- You may need to complete a *constat amiable* form (the other party may have one, or you might be able to get one from a *tabac* if there's one nearby). If you search the Internet for *'constat

amiable PDF' then you will find an example, so you can at least get an idea what they look like. Morocco being what it is, it seems far more likely you'll find yourself negotiating over whose fault it was, and what settlement they expect.
- If you do complete one, make sure you keep your copy of the *constat amiable*, and take a photo of the third party's insurance certificate or Green Card if possible.

Parking
Moroccan kerb stones are often painted in bright colours. Red and white stripes and green and white stripes are supposed to mean something, but we couldn't work it out as there were often people parked by both, so we joined them. If you spot someone in a high vis jacket, they're probably a *gardien*, and you'll need to pay them a few Dirhams to park there. Be sure to ask how much it will be before you park up as one cheeky guardian in Agadir wanted to charge us 50Dh (£4.50) to park outside a shop for half an hour. How much you should pay varies from place to place, but from our experience if they ask for anything over 5Dh (45p) we would go elsewhere. Outside of the cities and large towns, we found we could normally park in the town alongside the road for free. Marjane, and other large supermarkets, have a large car park with plenty of space for motorhomes.

Buying Fuel
Diesel and unleaded petrol are available across Morocco from European-style petrol stations with metered pumps, Shell and Afriqua being two of the bigger brands. Diesel is called *gasoil* (pronounced gaz-wal), and unleaded fuel is *essence* (pronounced ess-arnse). The diesel is of good quality, but if you do plan to travel into the mountains in winter, take note that it may not have winter additives in to prevent gelling in very low temperatures (-8°C or below). You can buy anti-gel additives before you come to Morocco, but we never needed them.

To buy fuel, drive up to the pump, checking it has your type of fuel. Turn off your engine and an attendant will come over to the driver's window and ask for the key to the fuel cap, if it needs one. You indicate how much fuel you want, either by telling them in French, by showing the value of the notes you want to spend (two 200Dh notes for example), or just asking for *plein* (pronounced plen) to get a full tank.

Some fuel stations will take credit cards, not all, so ensure you have enough cash to pay just in case. Hand the money to the attendant when they're done filling and they'll bring back any change. A tip of 3 to 5Dh is gratefully accepted by attendants.

The price of diesel and petrol jumped in 2014 when the Moroccan government removed the state subsidy on them. While we were there in 2012, diesel cost roughly 7.5Dh a litre (60p a litre). In 2021 the price is around 9Dh a litre (73p a litre), still cheaper than in Spain so arrive with an emptyish tank. If you want to get an idea of up to date fuel prices in the cities, have a look at *www.prix-carburant.ma*.

Using Taxis and Buses

Some campsites are located some distance out of town, especially in larger cities such as Fes and Marrakech. If you don't want to walk, cycle or drive into the centre of these cities, then some options available to you are:

- Use a tourist taxi arranged by the campsite. These are very easy to arrange, clean, safe but compared with other forms of transport, expensive.
- Use a guide. If you pay for a guide to take you around the cities (which we'd highly recommend for Fes), then they'll collect you from the campsite in their own vehicle or a tourist taxi and drop you off when the tour is complete.
- Ask the campsite to order you a *petit taxi*, or head out onto the street and flag one down. These only operate within urban areas, not between towns (*grands taxis* ply routes between towns), and can only take 3 passengers. If you use a petit taxi, tell the driver where you want to go and agree a price for all passengers before you set off. We used a tourist taxi to get to the start of a 10KM run we were doing in Fes and flagged down a petit taxi to get back. The tourist taxi was 100Dh for four people, the petit taxi 20Dh for two.

- Ask the campsite for the location of the nearest bus stop. These seem to be the cheapest option by far. When we tried to use one in Fes we simply couldn't find the bus stop, which the campsite had indicated was a few hundred metres walk away. A bus did pass us, but it was too full for anyone else to physically squeeze in the door.

Overnight Stays

Morocco is a very well-established destination for campervan and motorhome travellers. The *campercontact.com* website currently lists over 300 places to stay. While it's worth noting that Morocco isn't a country where free (wild) camping is generally tolerated, we've some anecdotal evidence that free camping is possible, particularly in the less visited locations or in less conspicuous vans. That's said, it's probably best to budget for campsites and treat the occasional free night as a bonus, rather than the other way around. Campsites or other official overnight stopovers are generally around £8.50 (€10) a night or less, including electricity, and you'll be travelling in a country where the locals very much need the income.

Options Available for Motorhome Stopovers

The following sections outline the types of overnight stopover locations available, how to find them, what to expect from them, and what not to expect. In practice there is no local formal categorisation system for places to stay. Some places won't fit into the categories below, and some will seem to fall into more than one.

How to Find Overnight Stops

We've already mentioned various campsite books and databases in the 'Preparation Before You Go' section. These tools will lay out overnight locations on a map to help you find somewhere to stay close to where you are going. We prefer the online databases and apps, such as *campercontact.com*, *park4night.com*, *ioverlander.com* and *campingcar-infos.com*, because in addition to the facilities and costs of a stop, they often have user-submitted photos of the site and the toilet/shower block, as well as reviews from fellow travellers. These reviews and photos are very helpful in getting an idea what the site is like and which to choose if there are more than one in a location.

Campsites

Moroccan campsites vary enormously in style and quality, from small walled compounds to open sites in the mountains or alongside the Saharan dunes. On first sight some of the walled sites can be intimidating. The walls are often over head height, and you wonder whether all this security is really necessary. Just like Morocco itself this feels intimidating at first, but it soon becomes clear that although some of the less scrupulous locals might overcharge you a few Dirhams here and there, very few thefts occur. When you realise this, it becomes obvious that the walls are there partly for security, but also to keep the weather out and provide some much-wanted shade. Occasional high winds (called the *chergui*) coupled with dusty or sandy ground can lead to air filled with dirt, and being alongside a high wall in that kind of weather is a blessing.

A pitch under palm trees at Campsite Oasis Palmier in Zagora

In paper format, J. Gandini's *Campings du Maroc* (French language only – you can get it from Amazon) is updated yearly and is an excellent reference source for Morocco's campsites, however it has no photos of them, no user-reviews, and doesn't list guarded parking locations, which is why we predominantly used offline versions of the online directories.

Like in Europe, campsites are typically on the edge of town, or some distance away from a town or village, and you'll see many French motorhomes with a second means of transport (moped or quad bike) to enable them to easily visit the local town and other attractions. Some sites will offer a tourist taxi, which will likely be a clean and fairly new people carrier, and will cost much more than local taxis (see 'Using Taxis and Buses' section). Push bikes are an option too, and despite Morocco's poor reputation for road safety, drivers gave us cyclists plenty of space when passing.

Faux Campsites

In addition to established campsites with dedicated parking areas and sanitary facilities for motorhomes, there are a large number of more informal campsites. You still pay for these, and they might call themselves *campings*, but they offer a different experience to campsites. Faux campsites have generally been established by the owners of restaurants and *auberges* (combined restaurant-hotels). We've used a few faux campings in Morocco and as long as we were aware of what we were getting, were happy with them.

The main areas which identify a faux campsite are:

- They have no dedicated toilet and shower block for motorhomes. You may find yourself being 'upgraded' to the facilities inside the main building.
- They have no dedicated facilities for black or grey water disposal. You may be able to dump black waste in a toilet, as directed by the staff.
- They may or may not have electrical hook-up. In one faux campsite at the Aït Benhaddou fortified village north-west of Ouarzazate, our friend's hook-up cable was lifted through a window into the adjacent building and plugged-in inside somewhere.
- They may or may not allow you to carry out 'camping behaviour', putting out your awning, chairs, table and so on. Each is different.
- They will probably charge less than a campsite, maybe only 40Dh or 50Dh, or you may be able to stay for free if you take a meal in the restaurant. You need to discuss and agree the price with the guardian or owner when you arrive.

Guarded or Guardian Parking

Guarded parking locations are basically the Moroccan equivalent of a European motorhome aire. They are formal parking areas, where the local authorities allow motorhomes to park overnight, and are often close to or even in the heart of cities. There are guarded parking locations in the centres of Marrakech, Fes and Mèknes, for example, and all are shared with cars and other vehicles. Campsite databases will usually list guardian parking locations, give GPS co-ordinates and an idea of price for overnight parking – which can range from very small amounts of 10Dh or 20Dh up to around 50 to 100Dh in the cities.

Despite the name, guarded parking locations shouldn't really be considered to be 'guarded' as such. The guardians are usually around during the day, but in the evening they go home. One or more men wearing high vis jackets will meet you on arrival, sometimes waving to you from a distance so you can see where to go, and they usually (but not always) take payment on arrival. They'll ask how many nights you want to stay for, and then give you a price. If they don't ask for payment on arrival, make sure you understand the price before parking up.

Guardian parking next to the Fes medina

Guarded parking locations will have no, or limited facilities for motorhomes. There may be somewhere to take on water, but usually nowhere to dispose of black or grey waste. You'll be expected to park reasonably close to the motorhomes next to you, and camping activities are not normally tolerated. Also, the official status of these locations varies over time seemingly depending on local politics: guarded parking areas we've used in Essaouira and Fes are currenting being reported as off-limits for overnight parking.

Our experience of guarded parking locations has been good. We've had no issues with safety or thefts, and anecdotal evidence from others was similar. As you're usually parked in the open, there is little to stop children begging at the door, or traders trying to sell you their goods. There's also likely to be some noise from roads, minarets, barking dogs and so on if you're close to or in a city.

Free or Wild Camping

In this book we'll use 'Free Camping' rather than 'Wild Camping', although the two terms are pretty much interchangeable and refer to parking outside officially-designated areas. We like to practice free camping where tolerated, in combination with using pretty much every other type of overnight stopover location. Speaking to people who'd travelled in Morocco some years ago, wild or free camping was easy and tolerated.

Free camping above the painted rocks near Tafraoute

Officially free camping is no longer tolerated in Morocco, and we've only done it in one location in the Anti-Atlas Mountains. That's not to say it's impossible; if you search the Internet or ask fellow travellers, you'll always find anecdotes of people who never use campsites in Morocco. Also, as with most countries the police aren't likely to be motivated to search out your remote parking spot in the hills and ask you to move. However, where there are campsites, faux campsites or guarded parking areas, you'll be generally expected to use them.

What Standards to Expect

Once you're in Morocco and off the motorway, it'll quickly become evident that standards are, erm, different to Europe. There's nothing to be fearful of, but you should expect a general deterioration in cleanliness. Standards in campsites will vary hugely, so the following sections should only be used as guidelines.

Price Lists

Most campsites have a price list shown at the door or in reception. The costs are often broken down so you can build up the nightly cost depending on how many people are in your party, number and size of vehicles, whether you want electricity and so on. The price lists usually have pictures so you don't need to translate French or Arabic. If the site offers discounts for longer stays, this is stated on the price list. Some sites charge extra for hot showers, typically around 10Dh. Also, if a site has a functioning and useable swimming pool, it may also be charged for.

Pets are normally allowed and are free of charge. Dogs are expected to be exercised off-site and kept on a lead on-site, although this is routinely ignored. There is no need or point in trying to haggle over the price list.

A campsite price list in Zagora

Pitches

Campsites are generally surfaced with gravel or, in some cases, packed sand. We carried a large plastic mat on our bike rack and rolled it out next to the van door when possible, making it more comfortable to walk around bare foot, and reducing the sand and dirt brought into the van. These mats are widely available in Morocco and much cheaper than in Europe or the UK.

A pitch at Camping Amasttou, in Tazzarine

Pitches are sometimes marked out, sometimes separated by foliage and sometimes you just park where you like. Some sites on the coast south of Agadir were very busy with over-wintering French motorhomes when we arrived in February, and we found you may have to stay outside reception for a night or two until a pitch becomes available.

As usual, even on campsites, pitches are not always level so it pays to bring ramps with you. Our friends also brought a small spade and found it easier to dig out holes for wheels rather than try to level out the ground with ramps.

Electricity

Electrical hook-up is 220V, so UK and European appliances will work. You will need a two pin Europlug (French style) adaptor for your electrical hook-up cable. Electricity is frequently reverse polarity (you may need to insert the plug on your cable upside down, or use an adaptor if you're worried about this) and sometimes has no earth. The sockets on campsites may be mounted in mud walls, on the sides of palm trees, on the tops of poles, you name it. They don't appear well protected by the weather, so take care in wet conditions.

Interesting electrics at Hotel Jurassique's campsite in the Ziz Gorge

Electrical capacity varies between four Amps to over 10 Amps, so be aware if you're using a kettle or hotplate at the same time as an electrical heater, you may overload the circuit. Although some sites quoted different prices for different maximum currents, none actually seemed to enforce this. Some outlets have RCD switches so you can reset them yourself, but otherwise you'll need to contact the site manager. Voltage variations appear on some sites, referred to as brown outs, so it might take an age to boil the kettle or your fan heater might sound like it's struggling a little.

A small number of more remote campsites disable the electricity overnight, and some have signs up stating that electrical heaters are forbidden. We ignored the heater signs as there were only a small number of people staying on these sites at the time, and we made sure we consumed less than four Amps, by switching off the electric heater before switching on the kettle, so we didn't trip the supply.

Almost all campsites have electricity available, and normally had plenty of outlets so there was no need to share outlets with neighbours or carry a long electrical cable.

Toilets

Toilets on campsites in Morocco include both squatter and European style. More often than not, there is no toilet paper so bring your own. Remember to place used loo roll into the basket provided rather than in the toilet; the Moroccan sewer system can't cope with it.

You might spot a length of silver hose hooked up next to the toilet: this is the local traditional way of cleansing yourself. Rather than using toilet paper you would use this hose to deliver water, and clean yourself with your left hand. This is why you shouldn't shake hands, touch people, eat or pick up food with your left hand when in public!

Showers

As our motorhome's shower uses gas to heat the water, by using on-site showers we managed to easily eke out our 17Kg LPG supply to last 3 months. It's also a pleasure to stand under an unlimited supply of hot water, however in Morocco nothing is guaranteed! Showers are sometimes hot at one time of day and not another (either solar heated, or the gas bottle attached to the boiler ran out). In some cases one shower will be hot, but not the others, or shower heads may be broken or missing so you end up with just a dribble of water. Which is the best shower is always a topic of conversation on campsites, but to be frank, some of them did feel like you've committed an offence bad enough to land you in a Columbian prison, they can be pretty raw.

In the more arid parts of the country, it makes sense to keep showers as short as possible. Taking a hot shower when stood next to the Sahara is an unforgettable experience, as your skin and hair starts to feel dry and parched, but keeping the water flowing can't be easy for the locals.

Grey Water

Some of the more modern campsites have a drive-over grey water disposal point. Most don't have anything, so you need to either bucket the water out to a drain or some thirsty-looking plants, or empty out by the road somewhere. While dumping grey water onto the ground in Europe is frowned upon, there are enough huge areas of desert in Morocco that it's really not an issue. One campsite we stayed on in M'hamid would pump out the adjacent hotel's grey water onto the plants around us each morning. It didn't smell nice, but water's precious down there, even used water.

Black Water (Toilet Cassette Emptying)

All campsites have a dedicated black water disposal point, included in the price of the campsite if you're staying there. They're all artisanal, so you'll come across a whole range of designs. They don't always have a water tap nearby to rinse the cassette, in which case you might want to use an old water bottle and take it with you.

Dumping black waste on the ground isn't acceptable anywhere. We only saw one place where it was being routinely done, at the huge municipal parking area at Tafraoute. There are plenty of campsites in the country, so there is no need to do it anywhere, and even in Tafraroute a nearby campsite (Camping Granite Rose) allowed black waste emptying for 20Dh for non-residents.

Fresh Water

Fresh water's available in all campsites and even in some guarded parking areas if you ask the guardian. The water may or may not be drinkable (*eau potable*), you need to ask and if you're not sure either boil it or chemically treat with purification tablets before drinking it. Bring a water carrier which you can use to fill your tank too, not all sites have a tap you can connect a hose to.

The NHS website recommends for travel to Morocco that "boiled and bottled water (with intact seal) is usually safe, as are hot tea and coffee, beer and wine." Most of the time we opted to use bottled water for drinking, which is widely available in 1.5 litre and 5 litre plastic bottles with sealed caps and prices printed on the labels. However, as the plastic bottles aren't widely recycled in Morocco, when we were certain the tap water was safe to drink, we would drink it. If we were unsure, we would use bottled water for cold drinks and tap water only when boiled or treated with chemical purifier tablets first.

Top Tip: Even if the water on the site is *potable*, it may still upset your stomach as it contains different chemicals and minerals to what you are used to. We found that by topping up a half empty bottle of bottled water with water from a tap, our stomachs got an easier introduction to the local water. After that we had no problems drinking from the *potable* water taps.

Rubbish Disposal

Out of necessity, Moroccans re-use practically everything. Old tyres are turned into buckets or shoe soles. Ancient clothes are piled into heaps in markets, alongside piles of unmatched shoes. Old mobile phone batteries and rubber keyboards are spread out in the souks for punters to look for a match. Plastic water bottles bought by us tourists to ensure safe drinking water are sometimes gathered together by kids and re-used or turned into plastic motorhome carpets.

However, what can't be re-used by the general population gets dumped as rubbish, and only 5% of all of Morocco's rubbish was recycled in 2016. Waste tips are much different to Europe. Expect the dumps to be located next to towns and open to the air. On larger dumps families will pick over the waste for anything they can sell.

You'll also see small piles of rubbish smouldering as locals attempt to deal with the problem themselves. Although this removes the waste, it obviously leaves behind a mess, and toxins from the smoke enter the food chain again through plants and then animals.

Sadly, you'll see rubbish strewn across much of Morocco

There isn't a great deal you can do about this but try to reduce, reuse and recycle where you can. Use the bins on campsites as industrial bins are few and far between. Sometimes you have to use smaller bins alongside pavements in towns. At least by using these the rubbish is contained and moved away from the general population. In a small number of locations you won't be able to find a bin, be prepared to bag up your rubbish and take it with you.

Swimming Pools

Campsite swimming pools are a source of black-humoured amusement among motorhome travellers. A handful of sites will have a clean, safe swimming pool available, although in winter few of them are warm enough to enjoy much time in. In places there is a charge for use of the pool, so ask before splashing. An equal number of sites will have a pool devoid of water, or will look like they last had water in a decade ago. Take care if travelling with children as there's nothing to prevent them, or us adults for that matter, from falling in.

An empty pool at Camping Zerhoun Bellevue near Moulay Idriss

On-Site Restaurants

Where a campsite has an on-site restaurant, you can be sure the staff will let you know about it. Our experience of Moroccan campsite restaurants has been overwhelmingly good. Menus are usually available, but if not just ask what there is. As ever, make sure you understand the cost before ordering, but the food is usually very good value. For example, chicken tagines are about 50Dh a person, rising to maybe 80Dh a person for a good fish tagine. You'll need to order between two and four hours' in advance if you want a slow-cooked dish such as a tagine. So it's always best to ask as soon as you arrive and don't expect to just turn up and eat.

Top Tip: As campsite restaurants are rarely heated and sometimes outdoors, wrap up well before you venture out to eat in the evening, or you can often choose to have your meal delivered to your motorhome.

A lamb tagine delivered to our motorhome at a campsite in Tafraoute

Clothes Washing

Some larger campsites, and those with hotel rooms, often have some type of laundry service. Either they'll have one or more washing machines you can use yourself, or they'll take your laundry and you collect it later from reception dried and folded. Prices are around 40Dh a load. You may need to provide your own washing liquid/powder and softener, so take it when you hand over your washing. Dryers are not available, which isn't usually an issue as the weather is frequently good enough to dry even jeans quickly on a line. Bring your own washing line and pegs, as not all sites have ones available to use.

On-Site Traders

On many campsites traders will arrive in cars and vans, on foot or even with a donkey throughout the day. They sell everything from bread, biscuits, Argan oil, honey, fruit and vegetables, fish, Berber jewellery, *harira* soup, the opportunity to have a Moroccan scene painted on your van, new windscreen wipers, plastic carpets, wheel covers, shoe holders, a haircut, solar panels, you name it. The prices are usually a bit higher than you'd pay in the souks or small grocery stores. The traders can be both a god-send and a daily annoyance, depending on how you're feeling at the time, and we found we preferred the campsites which had few on-site traders present.

Leaving Times

The vast majority of Moroccan campsites aren't used to enforcing rules. Some will state you have to leave by midday, but if you ask they may well let you stay a few hours longer. Most don't state a leaving time and you just go when you want to. People tend to leave in the morning, as drives can take a long time even if they aren't a long distance.

Registering Arrival – Fiches

When you arrive at a campsite the site manager should, by law, request you complete a registration *fiche* (pronounced feesh), much like the immigration form you completed to enter the country. They don't want this straight away, but will want it by the end of your first day. Some will want a form per person, some will be happy with one form per party, and some will just photocopy your passport and be happy with that. You only need to complete the fiche(s) on the first day you arrive somewhere.

Some Basics for Day-to-Day Life

Life in Morocco was an ever-present fascination to us. Every day would bring something new, some new sight, experience, sound or smell. The way in which day-to-day life is carried out has so many differences to the way we live in Europe, that Morocco can be an exhausting experience! The following sections aim to give you some insight into the way we experienced Moroccan life, in the hope they ease you into the place and help you enjoy it all the more.

Obtaining Currency – the Moroccan Dirham

Morocco is a cash economy. Some places will take credit cards, notably some petrol stations and the large supermarket chains (Marjane and Carrefour), but on the whole you'll be expected to deal in cash. Receipts are sometimes issued, but often are not, especially for smaller purchases.

Moroccan currency, the Dirham

At the time of writing (Dec 2019), tourist rates for Moroccan Dirhams are as follows – as a rough calculator when buying items, divide the Moroccan Dirham value by ten to get the price in Euros.

- 10 Moroccan Dirhams = 80 pence Sterling
- 10 Moroccan Dirhams = €0.94

Moroccan Dirhams (shortened to Dh in this book) come in notes:
- 200Dh (about £16, €20)
- 100Dh (about £8.50, €10)
- 50Dh (about £4, €5)
- 20Dh (about £1.60, €2)

And coins, 10Dh (about 80p , €1), 5Dh (about 40p , €0.5), 1Dh (about 8p, €0.10) and smaller 'centime' coins (100 centimes make up a Dirham). While centimes are often included in prices, the total can be rounded up or down, so we didn't actually see these coins until we were in the south of the country.

Top Tip: Buying items in Morocco can be an adventure in itself! It's easy to get confused and think a seller's charging you ten times what an item is worth. Stay cool folks (unlike us), if he wants 20Dh for that huge bag of fruit and veg, it's only £1.60 (€2), not £16 (€20).

Once you're inside Morocco, Dirhams can be widely obtained from cash machines. We relied mainly on our Halifax Clarity credit card, which had no transaction fees, offered a reasonable exchange rate but did charge interest on cash taken out. Normally, in Europe, we'd use a pre-loaded Caxton FX card, but this couldn't be loaded with Moroccan Dirhams (we later found this could be loaded with Sterling and should have worked in Morocco, but we never tried this). Our normal bank debit card worked, but the fees and exchange rate made it more expensive than the Halifax card.

The Many Languages of Morocco

First the good news: you can get by in Morocco without speaking the local lingo. In fact, you can get by anywhere in the world without speaking the language. But, as always, the more you know, the easier and more interesting life will be. Moroccans officially speak dialects of Arabic and Berber. In written form, the two alphabets compare to our Roman alphabet like this:

Roman: Azrou

Arabic: أزرو

Berber: ⵓⵥⵔⵓ

The Roman version of the place name 'Azrou' was created by someone taking the Arabic and/or Berber place name and trying to make the same sounds using the 26-character Roman alphabet. This is called transliteration, and it's not always accurate, as Berber and Arabic have sounds which the Roman alphabet does not. Different translators also use different Roman letters to represent the same sound, explaining why places names vary between different books, maps, websites and so on.

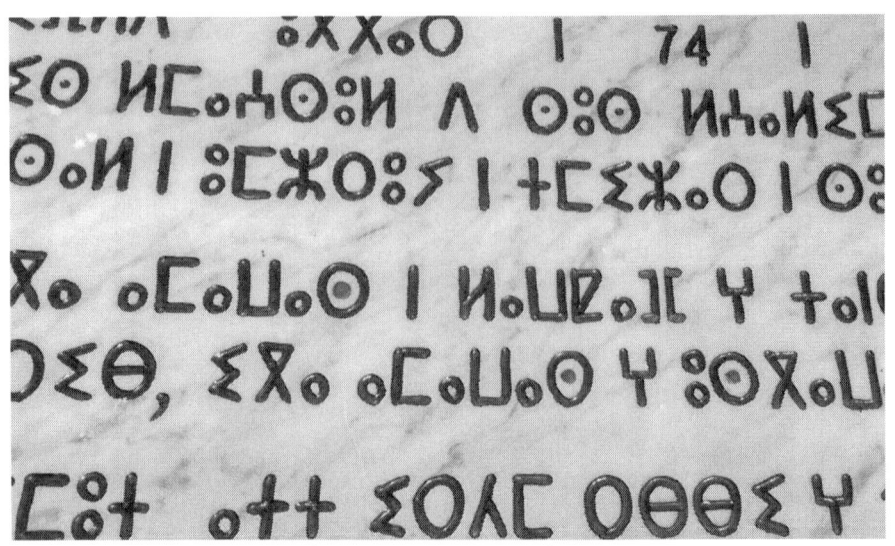

Berber script at a sign in Tafraoute

For most of us, these alphabets are completely alien. Fortunately, many Moroccans also speak French, some fluently and some not much more than basic phrases and numbers. Most signs across the country have a French translation, giving us a chance of understanding them! So if you have some French, you're at an advantage, but even if you don't you will be able to navigate the country and deal with the locals.

A handful of signs are in Arabic only, but even with this one there was a French one nearby

While we can't read Arabic, we did memorise some basic Arabic phrases. We found there was no backlash from using French, a language introduced by a foreign empire, but when we used Arabic words we'd often get a smile. It was worth the small amount of effort we put in. Some of the more useful Arabic phrases we learned were:

- *Shukran* – thanks
- *La* – no
- *Na'am* - yes
- *La Shukran* – no thanks – you'll use this one a fair bit…
- *Salaam* – the short version of hello – we only used this
- *Bessalama* – bye!
- *Salaam Alaykum* – the long version of hello
- *Labas?* – how are you
- *Labas* – I'm fine
- *Wakha* – OK

There are more Moroccan Arabic phrases at *speakmoroccan.com*. Varying spellings and use of some different words is common. The words and pronunciations above worked for us.

Insh'Allah

You're bound to come across the small, but hugely important phrase insh'allah. It's widely used in Morocco, and somehow tied up in the national psyche. Its literal meaning is 'God Willing' but in day-to-day use has a far more nebulous meaning. Depending on the context, it seems to mean either 'maybe', 'if you're lucky', 'I don't know', 'I hope so' or 'there's no chance the thing we're talking about is ever going to happen'. Working out which one applies at any one time is a lot of fun. Some examples:

"Tomorrow you will come to my carpet shop, insh'allah"

"You are married, but you have no children? You will have them soon, insh'allah"

"Your camper van has broken down? We will get it fixed, insh'allah"

"We will complete this building project on time, insh'allah"

Guides

Guiding tourists around cities, towns and attractions is an important source of income for many Moroccans. In a country where millions live on a few pounds a day, a guide earning 300Dh for a day's tour (about £24) will be relatively well off. Given this opportunity to earn good money, in the past thousands of Moroccans declared themselves as guides, regardless of their level of knowledge, ability to speak European languages or use of a safe vehicle. To tackle this problem the government created a licensing system, and declared any unlicensed guides (referred to as faux guides) to be illegal and subject to arrest. This may have reduced the problem, but certainly hasn't stopped it.

> We decided to visit the town of Moulay Idriss, and found ourselves being waved into a parking space by what we took to be the guardian. After a negotiation over the parking price, we got out and started to walk towards the town. The guardian walked alongside us, asking various questions about where we came from, what we wanted to see and so on. Starting to suspect he might be a faux guide, we told him we didn't want a guided tour, and he brushed off the suggestion and carried on walking with us.
>
> And that was that, whether we wanted a guide or not we had one. Going by the name of Idriss, he knew little English, mainly kept to the outskirts of the town, and engaged in some verbal abuse with other Moroccans (who we guessed knew he was operating illegally) when he took us to try and peer into the famous mosque. At the end of the 45 minute 'tour', he demanded 150Dh from us.
>
> Unhappy that we'd been duped, we handed over 50Dh, but he made it clear this wasn't enough, demanding we give him two boxes of wine, which we did to get rid of him, and vowed never to get caught out by using a poor quality faux guide again. Since then when a local has attempted to attach themselves to us (some of which are children), we've politely stopped and confronted them, telling them we don't want a guide, and just want to walk on our own, waiting until they acknowledge we really don't want them.

Professional, licensed guides can transform your experience of cities. They can talk you through their history and culture. The best will take you to see into small but fascinating corners, like a junior school classroom or the sawdust burning room for a *hammam* (a traditional Moroccan communal bath house). They will act as a kind of shield against faux guides, beggars and other people who would otherwise bother you as you look around. They can be a fantastic source of local information, answering all your questions about how life in Morocco works, Islam, family life and so on.

Guides in Fes, even the best professional ones, will take you to a series of craft workshops and shops during the day, such as shoe-makers, potters, *zellij* (tile workers), carpet weavers, or metal pattern hammerers. They do this to allow you to see craftsmen at work, to give themselves a break for eating or prayers during the day, and to get a kick-back for anything you buy in the shops. While agreeing a price with the guide you can make it clear up front if you don't want to buy from shops. They'll take you anyway, as the shops are an integral part of the tours they do, but if the sell gets too hard you can remind them of your earlier conversation.

Finding a good guide is a case of asking around. Campsites will normally have one or more guides 'attached' to them who will visit the site to pick up and drop off clients. Asking other motorhomers at your campsite should give you a good idea whether a guide is a good one and give you some idea of price. Note that few guides speak good English, so unless your French or German is good, you need to be sure you'll be able to converse with them. The cost for an English-speaking guide may be slightly higher than a French speaker.

> We've used professional guides twice in Fes, both arranged through the campsite reception. In 2012 the tour was arranged by a French motorhomer we'd met earlier in the day. The guide was very good at showing our group around the corners of the city, but because the rest of the group were French, the majority of the tour was in French so we only understood parts of it. It only cost 250Dh (around £20) for both of us for a full day's tour, plus a contribution to the guide's lunch and a tip, which we thought good value.
>
> In 2017 we arranged the guide ourselves based on a recommendation by another British motorhomer at the site. They vouched for the guide and said his English was good. Initially the guide quoted 600Dh for four people, which he reduced to 500Dh (around £40) when we asked for a reduction. He was again very good, and well worth the money.

Tourist Information Offices

We were unable to find any useful tourist information offices while in Morocco (we soon gave up trying). We expect that the big cities will have them, but we decided to make use of guidebooks, forums, fellow travellers, professional guides and campsite staff to inform ourselves about the places we visited instead.

Tourist Police

We found Morocco to be a safe country to visit, even the larger cities in many ways felt safer than European towns and cities. We did take note of the *Brigade Touristique* (tourist police) who have a very visible presence in the famous Djeema el-Fna square in Marrakech and are on hand if feel you're being mistreated. If you do feel unhappy with a person aggressively begging from you, or an overzealous shop keeper, mentioning that you'll go and speak to the Brigade Touristique may help ease or end the situation.

Accidents

This is Africa. The pavements, where they exist, will have the occasional man-sized hole for you to fall into. Curbs are high and uneven. Bare wires poke out of all kinds of electrical installations. Edges of roads drop away, marked out only with a small pile of rocks. The country isn't a death trap, but requires a higher level of self-awareness and common sense than you'd normally find in Europe. In some ways it is quite refreshing to look after yourself. If you do find yourself injured or in need of assistance, the Moroccan people will help you, even if they can't speak the same language. We spoke to a fellow traveller who fell off his bicycle and was quickly surrounded by people trying to help him. There are doctors, pharmacies and dentists in every major town and the campsite owner will be able to help you if you need to get an appointment.

Holes in the pavement aren't unknown in Morocco

Swimming in Fresh Water

Schistosomiasis or bilharzia is a parasite which lives in fresh water and enters your body through the skin. The NHS suggests "avoidance of swimming, bathing or paddling in fresh water lakes and streams". As we didn't fancy a parasite, you can be sure we followed the NHS advice.

Shopping

Buying Food and Drink

Rough Ideas for Prices

As rough idea for basic items you might buy:

- 5 litre bottle of drinking water – 10 to 12Dh
- 1 flat round loaf of bread – 1.2 to 2Dh
- 1Kg minced steak – 80Dh
- 6 eggs – 9Dh
- A carrier bag of mixed fruit & vegetates from a souk – 20 to 40Dh
- 1Kg of caramelised nuts – 40Dh
- 1Kg of dates – 40Dh
- 1Kg of olives – 15Dh

Supermarkets

Morocco has a few supermarket chains, with Marjane and Carrefour being the largest and most obvious as you drive past. You may see them referred to as hypermarkets, but they're typically the size of a standard supermarket in the UK. The shops offer fixed prices and a fairly broad range of Western goods, but only the Carrefour supermarkets will sell a range of alcoholic drinks. Supermarkets offer a sanitised shopping experience, which can be both a little boring, and a relief after shopping the more intense, authentic way in souks and small grocery shops.

The Marjane supermarket in Agadir

Grocery Shops

There are tiny grocery shops everywhere. You can walk into a few of the larger ones and pick the items you want. More often than not there is a counter that the vendor sells items over, which means you have to tell them what you want. Some will speak French, so if you know what you want in that language you can get by. Otherwise you're into the realm of pointing and using your fingers to show how much you want or ask if you can go behind the counter and look around. These places look intimidating at first, but we've only ever had good experiences buying from them and have been behind the counter of quite a few.

Grocery shops sell everything in Morocco and some even let you play at shop keeper!

Fruit and Vegetable Shops

You'll sometimes find the fruit and vegetable shops in the municipal market area of a town, if you can't track one down the weekly souks are also a great place to stock up. Simply grab one of the old washing up bowls and go around the store putting in what you want. When you are done go to the chap with the weighing scales. He'll check what is in the bowl and remove any of the more expensive items such as avocados. Everything else left in the bowl then gets weighed together in the bowl, this means that potatoes, tomatoes, carrots and the like are all the same price per kilo.

Don't be surprised if a few extra onions or carrots go into your bowl to make it up to the next full kilo. If you have only had 'bowl price' goods, the weighing scales man may then move on and serve several other people while you stand there and wait to pay. We never got to the bottom of this, but assume it is because you are expected to know how much it will be based on how much it weighs. Catch his eye and ask him how much it is: *combien*? (com-bee-ann).

Buying fresh fruit and vegetables

Butchers

The traditional Moroccan butchers is a sight to behold. There are split into two types – chicken and red meat, and are often grouped together so you will see a line of five red meat butchers shops in a row. The red meat butchers will have carcases of goats and cows hanging up in front of, or inside the shop, and might have the odd head or set of feet sat around, so a visit to them isn't always for the squeamish. Most red meat butchers have a price list showing the per-Kg costs, which might only be Arabic but is sometimes in French, and sometimes even has pictures of the various cuts so you can just point at it and say how much you want - *un demi kilo* (pronounced ern derme-keelo, ½ a kilo) is usually plenty for two people and for two or three meals!

A Moroccan butcher

The chicken shops usually kill and prepare chickens to order, so be prepared to look your dinner in the eye. The chickens are often stored outside the shop in cages and the smell generally isn't pleasant, so hold your nose as you walk past. If you don't fancy a still warm, super fresh chicken, then hunt around as some shops sell prepared chickens and/or chicken pieces retrieved from a fridge, or stock up when you find a supermarket. Chicken shops may also sell eggs, as will some small grocers, however the eggs will come in a plastic bag. Hold onto your egg box as you only get these in the supermarkets.

> We wanted to try some goat meat, so headed over to a street-facing butchers which had a few forlorn-looking decapitated goat heads outside (while this might sound gruesome, it soon becomes the norm). We asked for *chèvre* (French for goat, pronounced share-vra). The butcher held up what looked like a goat leg and thigh, and not having a clue what cut we wanted we nodded. He placed the entire thing onto the scales, but it was twice what we wanted so we got his attention and made a 'we wanted a smaller piece' hand gesture. He hacked the leg in half and returned to the electronic scales, which we watched like hawks trying to suss what the cost would be. He took out a calculator and tapped it a bit, then asked for 60Dh, which bore no resemblance to the numbers on the scales. We checked in supermarkets later and the price was correct. The goat went into a tagine, which we cooked for 5 hours with some dates and vegetables and it was tender and delicious.

Weekly Souks

Weekly souks take part in most towns across Morocco, sometimes twice a week. They are a great place to stock up on fruit and veg, dates, nuts and olives and for a look around at local life. For non-food items we found that souk sellers will tell you a price and there is little or no haggling about it, but the price is usually a fair one and the same as the locals will pay. The stalls can be packed with everything or just have a few old rusty tools on a blanket, and everything in between.

Some towns even have the day of the souk embedded in their name. The small town of Souk-el-Had-d'Afella-Irhir for example, south of the Aït Mansour gorge, is named –el-Had as it has a Sunday market. Look out for these days in place names:

- Souk-el-Had: Sunday souk
- Souk-el-Tnine: Monday souk
- Souk-el-Tlat (sometimes Souk-Tleta): Tuesday souk
- Souk-el-Arba: Wednesday souk
- Souk-el-Khemis: Thursday souk
- Souk-el-Jemaa: Friday souk
- Souk-el-Sebt: Saturday souk

Buying olives from a souk in Sidi Ifni

Old tools for sale in the Azrou souk

Road-Side Traders

As you drive along most roads except motorways you'll see road-side sellers, operating from small stalls, the backs of vans or even just a pile of rocks. They'll be selling whatever's produced locally, so you may see a line of vans selling nothing but dried figs, or just piles upon piles of oranges. Although we've made the odd purchase from these traders, it was often difficult to find somewhere to pull a motorhome in safely from the road.

Buying Alcohol

Being an Islamic country, your opportunities for buying alcohol are fairly well hidden, the choice is limited and it is expensive. This is why so many motorhome tourists choose to load up in Europe and bring it with them. Most Carrefour supermarkets will sell it and have a reasonable range. Some restaurants in more tourist-frequented areas will sell it and some hotels will sell it, even for taking off-premises in some cases.

The choice will probably be limited to two or three Moroccan produced lagers (Spéciale Flag, Stork or the more expensive Casablanca). There may also be a couple of Moroccan wines, mainly red but you may come across *vin gris* – grey wine – made from red grapes but when crushed the juice is removed from the skins so it doesn't take on the full red colour or taste.

A supermarket 'alcohol' selection by the cordials, all 0% and from 17Dh for a small can

On our second tour we'd run out of beer, so we asked the campsite manager at Zagora where we could buy some. He offered to source it for us and later that day a chap arrived on a moped with a carrier bag. It was discretely handed over to us and was chilled. While buying alcohol is expensive at the best of times in Morocco, this was eye-wateringly expensive once the campsite owner, delivery man and hotel it came from had all added their bit. A small can of Flag beer was 50Dh (£4 / €5) and a small bottle of Casablanca 80Dh (£7 / €8).

Bartering and Haggling

If the thought of bartering or haggling over anything makes you feel uncomfortable, don't worry, you are not the only one. The essentials of fuel, food and campsites are all fixed prices, you don't haggle over them, so all you need for day-to-day life can be bought without any dispute over prices.

What's the Difference?

Bartering is swapping one type of good or service for another. Money may be involved to make up a difference in agreed values, but it's not the main item of value in the transaction. Haggling is the process of negotiating over the price of goods or a service.

The Ethics

There is an argument that Europeans shouldn't haggle over the price of items in Morocco but should pay whatever price is suggested by the vendor. The argument goes on to say that we Europeans are so relatively wealthy we shouldn't try and reduce the vendor's income by forcing them to sell an item for a price lower than initially quoted. Our view on this is as follows:

- We agree that Europeans shouldn't haggle over certain items, since no-one haggles over them, locals or Europeans - see below.
- Haggling is part of the culture of Morocco, so for items which are haggled over by the locals, it feels right to us for Europeans to also haggle.
- Moroccans are brought up in an environment where haggling is the norm, Europeans are generally not, so Moroccan vendors are expert hagglers. Even if you go all out, and despite what the vendor might tell you about how you're getting the item for less than they bought it for, they won't lose money in the transaction. They're too good.

What to Haggle Over, and What Not to

Exactly what items you should and should not haggle over is a grey area, and a source of constant learning for us. You don't need to haggle over diesel or petrol, campsite fees (unless you're in a faux campsite or some other parking location where no price list is shown), anything priced up in supermarkets, food in souks, food from shops (which is not normally priced up), bottled water, motorway tolls, fruit juice drinks or food from street stalls, food in cafes or meals from restaurants. In all these cases, as in Europe, you look at it, ask for the price and if you don't want to pay it, you don't consume the goods or service, there is no argument, it's easy.

It is traditional to haggle over more expensive one-off purchases like leather, pot, metal or wood crafts, although you can still avoid this by using the government-run fixed price *Ensemble Artisanal* shops in cities (ask your campsite reception where to find them). These are a collection of local craftspeople selling their goods direct. Often you can see them working to make the goods, and they are happy for you to talk with them and sometimes photograph them as they work.

Babouche (slippers) in the Marrakech souk, a haggle for these will get the price down a little

If you want to haggle over something, which can be a fun experience if you let it, here are some points to consider:

- Try and get an idea for the market value of similar items before you go to buy. Look around an Ensemble Artisanal, where many items are priced, although they do tend to be a little above souk prices, check out larger supermarkets in the big cities, or ask fellow travellers what they paid.
- Work out how much you want to pay for the item, what is it worth to you? In some cases we made sure we only had that amount of money in our pockets, so we couldn't get carried away.
- There are no rules around the price quoted by the seller and the final price they will accept. We heard that you should offer a third of their initial price to start with, but in practice that was rarely correct. Sometimes sellers will just state the exact price they want, especially for lower priced items in souks like hand tools, and will refuse to lower it. Sellers seem to weigh up buyers based on the way you're dressed, your hair cut, any jewellery you're wearing and so on, and set their prices accordingly.
- As the buyer you shouldn't state a price any higher than the one you're willing to pay. Sellers understandably get miffed if you tell them a price and then refuse to pay it.
- Be prepared to walk away. Although this can be a tactic for getting sellers to come down more on price, more often than not they'll not come after you.
- Have patience. Like many things in Morocco, things take longer than they do in Europe. You may need to go through a number of haggles with different sellers to get the price you want to pay.

What to Barter With

Normally money is used in transactions, but you might find yourself in a situation where you have the opportunity to swap items you have for items you want. A typical example for motorhome travellers seems to be push bikes, which you may be asked if you're willing to sell or swap for local goods like blankets, coats, Berber jewellery and so on. Other items we were asked for included clothes, shoes, mobile phones and any other electronic goods.

Moroccan Regional Specialities

Something to note while you're travelling around Morocco is that certain regions specialise in certain, locally available goods. If you wait to buy from these, you should get a better choice and a better price. For example, Fes is famous for leather goods, handbags, shoes and so on. Tafraoute is known for *babouche* (pronounced bab-oosh, leather slippers and shoes). The areas around Rissani abound with fossil sellers. Argan oil's produced and sold across the south-west of Morocco.

Improvements to Your Motorhome

Morocco has built up something of a reputation in motorhome circles as a place to get low cost alterations and improvements made to your vehicle. Typical services offered by the locals include reupholstering, repainting, fitting solar panels and painting typical Moroccan scenes onto various bits of your motorhome exterior. We've not had any of these done, but are worth at least considering if you need any of them. As with most businesses, good ones go bad and bad ones close, so probably best to consult the forums or ask around once you're in Morocco to get recommendations on suitable places to use, the level of quality to expect and prices.

A Moroccan motif painted on the side of a motorhome in Sidi Ifni

Eating Out

The NHS suggests you wash hands before eating and after using the toilet, and ensure clean dishes and utensils are used. If buying from street vendors, you should ensure the food is freshly cooked at a high temperature and freshly served. Foods to be cautious with: cheese and ice cream, often made from unpasteurised milk. Fish and shellfish, can be hazardous at all times of the year and best avoided if in doubt. Salads and fresh herbs (including in drinks) – should be avoided as "easily contaminated by soil or flies and are difficult to clean". Fruit, including tomatoes, should be peeled, and berries (in particular raspberries) "maybe a source of Cyclospora infection. They are difficult to wash and are best avoided."

We applied some of these rules but with a degree of common sense, we drank from fresh fruit drink stalls, and ate out frequently at a range of street sellers, cafés and restaurants, including a huge platter of fish and shellfish, with no ill effects.

Street Food

We've eaten street food across Morocco and have always enjoyed it. The food was mostly BBQ'd meat, either served on skewers or wrapped in half a round of bread, and was hot, cheap (typically 10Dh to 20Dh each), delicately flavoured and delicious. We've also eaten fish and chips a few times and although it's not the same as British fish 'n' chips, it was still delicious. Note that you may be offered a red sauce with your food, this is not ketchup, it is harissa – it's a fairly spicy concoction!

Buying street food in Fes

You'll also find fruit juice sellers who squeeze the fruit into a glass as you wait. Typically, a glass of fresh orange juice from a street vendor stall would be 4Dh, other fruits, including sugar cane or a mixture of fruits, were 10Dh a glass.

Restaurants

Moroccan restaurants don't tend to have a massive selection of dishes, but are generally good value. Most of our restaurant eating was done in campsite restaurants (see 'Overnight Stays' section earlier in this book), but we did eat out several times when were parked close to a town.

Typical choices in a restaurant will be – brochette (skewered meat), omelette, tagine and cous cous and unless you are in an auberge or hotel restaurant, drinks will nearly always be soft drinks only.

Top Tip: On our first trip in 2012, we had several experiences of cold chips being served with our food, so in 2017 we always made a point of checking they would be hot by asking for *pomme frites chaude* (pronounced pomm freet chowd).

Restaurants in tourist areas tend to clump together, so you may find yourself fending off a steady stream of menu touting waiters trying to get your business. Make sure you understand the cost and what is included before sitting down and ordering.

Food stalls

Pretty unique to Djeema el-Fna in Marrakech, food stalls are set up at dusk, pumping out noise, smoke and delicious smells, it's an experience you're not likely to forget in a hurry. As you approach the stalls you're almost certain to find yourself face-to-face with several menu touts, earnestly encouraging you to use their establishment. They use a mixture of cajoling, physically being in the way and humour to get you to sit down, we were even offered a 100% no diarrhoea guarantee by one of them! If you manage to shake the first lot off, you'll only get a few more metres before facing the next set of touts. This can be stressful, annoying, bewildering and a lot of fun.

If you get chance to actually look at the stalls as you're walking through, you'll see stalls selling goat heads, snails or bread stuffed with boiled eggs. The tourist stalls are more expensive, and sell a whole range of foods, which they cook fresh over coals or gas fires.

Top Tip: Try to get a seat away from the walkway if you can, towards the back of the stall where the food is, which will provide some insulation from the beggars and sellers who'll otherwise constantly interrupt your meal.

Eating at a food stall in Djeema el-Fna

Staying in Touch with Home

You might be surprised to learn that Morocco has excellent mobile phone and data networks. Almost everywhere in the country, as long as you're not in the middle of the desert in a 4x4 maybe, you'll be able to get a phone signal, and usually you'll have a 3G or better Internet data signal. Having Internet access allowed us to stay in touch with friends at home, and fellow travellers in Morocco, as well as being able to update the *ourtour.co.uk* travel blog as we went.

Buying an Internet SIM

Both times we visited Morocco we used the Maroc Telecom network (which appears as IAM on your phone). Maroc Telecom are the largest mobile provider in Morocco and have dedicated shops in many towns and cities across the country although be aware these shops operate a ticket queuing system, and wait times can be long. You can tell the shops by their blue and orange signage. You will also see many small shops with a small Maroc Telecom sign on the wall outside, that are selling other products. These are where you can buy top ups from, but they won't be able to help you buy a SIM.

A Maroc Telecom shop in Merzouga

Mobile network offers change quickly. When we first visited the country, we bought a USB dongle and SIM card with unlimited data for a month for 200Dh, and it took seconds to buy. On our second visit no unlimited plans were available so we bought 10GB of data for use over a 1 month period (without the USB dongle) for 100Dh, and with queueing and paperwork it took about an hour to buy it (prices are the same in 2021). We used this English language website to find out the latest information on the network providers, and what pre-pay packages and costs are available: *prepaid-data-sim-card.wikia.com/wiki/Morocco*.

Maroc Telecom allow pre-pay Internet SIM cards to be shared out (tethered) via a personal WiFi hotspot on a smart phone or MiFi-type device. However, we did find that Maroc Telecom SIMs would only work for a few minutes in our Huawei personal WiFi device. We brought this up with Maroc Telecom at their shop in Marrakech, but the assistant was unable to work out why the SIM wouldn't work in our device. To get around the problem we put the Maroc Telecom data SIM into one of our phones and shared the network from there. We also met other travellers using MiFi-type devices with a Maroc Telecom SIM with no issues.

To get connected to the Maroc Telecom network, follow these steps:

1. Ensure you have an unlocked device to place the Maroc Telecom SIM into. If your phone, tablet or MiFi is locked to a UK network, it won't work with a Moroccan SIM.
2. Find a Maroc Telecom shop, and take both your passport and the device you want to use the SIM in with you, as well as the cash in Dirhams to pay for the SIM and data.
3. If the shop is operating a queuing system, take a ticket for sales and wait your turn.
4. When your number comes up, go to the counter and tell them you need an Internet SIM. Some of the shops have English speaking staff, but if not try using a translation app, such as Google Translate and type in what you want. Show them the device you plan to use the SIM in, and tell them how much data you want to buy, so they can ensure you get the correct sized SIM and pre-pay package. In 2017 some Maroc Telecom SIM cards were not made to be cut down to the right size, so our friends

with iPads needed a different SIM, and a different offer to the ones we got.
5. The operative will photocopy your passport, and complete a series of forms on your behalf. Sign them as needs be.
6. When they give you the SIM, before leaving the counter, place it into your device and ensure it connects to the Internet. For some devices, like iPads, a process has to be carried out to activate the SIM card, best left to the technical staff in the shop.

Topping up SIM Data

Maroc Telecom doesn't have a website where you can track your data use. Make note of the date the SIM was activated, and make use of any in-device function you have to meter the data you're using, that way you'll know when the data/time period is running out. The process to buy top-ups is relatively simple:

1. Go to any shop which sells Maroc Telecom top-ups (called "Pass Jawal Internet"). There are plenty of them in most towns, marked out by a small orange and blue sign above the shop. Take the cash in Dirhams to buy the top-up, and ideally also the mobile phone number of the SIM, which comes on the packaging (we just took all of our packaging and paperwork).
2. If you speak French or Arabic tell them you want to buy an Internet top-up and how much you want to spend. If you don't speak either of those languages, simply write down the amount of data you want to buy in GB, show them how much money you want to spend and the packaging for the SIM.
3. There are two ways your SIM can be topped-up:
    a. The vendor can give you a small slip with a scratch-off area on the back (see below). You scratch off the number and follow the instructions in French. The process is to send a text message from your device which has the SIM in it to 555. The content of the message should be the scratched-off number, followed by a * symbol and the number 3. A text message will come back in French and/or Arabic confirming that the top-up has been successful.

b. You can give the vendor the phone number of the SIM, and they can use their phone to top-up the SIM for you – there is sometimes a small charge for this.

A 100Dh Maroc Telecom top-up voucher

Top Tip: When we needed to top up for the first time we took with us the packaging of the SIM we had to ensure we got a data top-up and not credit for voice and SMS messages. After that, we just took our previous top up voucher with us to get one the same.

Using your Phone in Morocco

We both use UK-registered SIMs when travelling in Europe to make calls and send texts. In Morocco the European caps on roaming charges for calls and text messages do not apply and making and receiving calls or SMS text messages is expensive. As of 2021, the cost to use our *1pmobile.com* SIMs to contact the UK from Morocco is £1 per minute to make and receive calls to UK landlines and mobiles. It costs £0.25 to send a text but they're free to receive. Mobile data on this SIM is 20p per MB in Morocco (£200 per GB).

We chose not to use our UK phone SIMs and stayed in touch using VOIP-type services like Skype to make and receive video and voice calls when on WiFi, or when we had data left towards the end of our top up. We also used other Internet services like Facebook Messaging or WhatsApp to send text or picture messages. If this isn't an option for you, we suggest talking to Maroc Telecom or another local network provider about a voice package. Be careful to ensure you understand the per-second call charges, as they may still be high for International calls.

Sending Post

Poste Maroc is Morocco's state-run postal service, and their offices are easily spotted in towns and cities by their bright yellow livery. They'll have a La Poste or PTT sign outside. We sent post cards and letters from Morocco, which arrived in the UK after a week or so. The stamps (*timbre* in French, pronounced tam-brer) were available from either the Poste Maroc offices or, in some cases, from small tabac shops. Remember to take the item you want to post with you, so it can be weighed if needed, and to say you need to send the mail to the UK, or whichever country, so they give you the correct value of stamps.

The Lonely Planet has more information on sending mail here: *www.lonelyplanet.com/morocco/post*. This also describes the Post Restante service – where you can have mail or parcels sent to the address of a post office while you're travelling, and pick the post up using your passport to identify yourself, however we never used this service.

Confusions and Annoyances

On entering Morocco for the first time, prepare yourself for a little culture shock. It might not be immediately apparent, but if you find your eye starting to twitch, a burning need to tell people how to do things better, or a slight fog of confusion and panic descend upon you, rest assured, you're not the first. Unless you've travelled in similar countries, various aspects of being in Morocco are probably going to take you aback, they did us. We've tried to run through some of them below, so you're better prepared to work out why your shoulders are feeling a bit tight and your eyes have gone a little wider than normal. The reasons below could explain why you might feel like you want to leave after just a few days in the country.

First Some Perspective

Please, please, please keep all of the stuff below in perspective. Morocco is a safe country. Travel and tourism support 1 in 11 Moroccan jobs and contributes roughly 10% of Morocco's GDP, so the industry is clearly of enormous importance to the country, and its people. Despite what mainstream media and politicians might imply in the Western World, your average Muslim Moroccan is a caring individual, who doesn't give two hoots whether you're also a Muslim or not. Once you've been to Morocco and returned back to Spain, you may find yourself surprised that, as well as suddenly finding life less colourful, you feel just a little less safe.

Your Newfound Rockstar Status!

Driving about in a motorhome in most of Europe is, unless you're about to wedge the thing down some medieval alleyway, not something which attracts much attention. Similarly you can walk down any street across the whole continent without folks as much as flicking their eyes at you, the strangers in town. Once you're in Morocco though, you're suddenly a rock star folks, and you'll soon get an idea what the famous must feel like walking the streets back home.

When driving your motorhome, expect waves of greetings from shepherds, school kids, women carrying loads along the road, you name it. Expect men, women and children to stand staring at you as you pass, sometimes lifting a hand in request for a lift. When you pull in somewhere, expect a face to appear at the door or window, ready to request some details about you, and subsequently flog you something. When walking down the street, expect to find eyes staring at you. Expect calls of "bonjour! ça va? hello! wie geht's?" and even to be whistled to get your attention. Expect men to wander up to you and run through the usual set of questions "Hello, where you from? First time in Morocco? Looking for something? I have a shop…"

Yep, the anonymity you didn't even realise you had in Europe is removed within hours of being in Morocco. How you deal with it's up to you, but we find we can cope with it as long as we have the ability to take refuge in campsites for a few days at a time. A few tips for handling this newfound status:

- Greeting people with a friendly *salaam* will (almost) always result in a salaam being said back to you in a show of mutual respect. *Salaam* (pronounced sal-arm) is Arabic for 'peace', and if you want to be a little more formal you can go for *Salaam Alaykum*, (pronounced sal-arm allay-kum), peace be with you.
- Gangs of young Moroccan men suddenly flip from malicious looking would-be muggers to broad smiling faces and waves, you just have to smile and hold up a hand in greeting first.
- If asked if this is your first time in Morocco, consider lying if it is! If you say you've been a few times, they'll know you're not green, and will be easier to dispatch if you don't want what they're selling.
- Touching your hand to your heart's a useful way to show someone you respect them.
- Keep patience at all times. Which can be easier said than done.

Beggars

There are many different types of beggar in Morocco. Their presence is a constant reminder of how lucky we are, and a constant ethical dilemma. Which should you give to? Should you give to any, considering others in nearby fields are working very hard to earn just a few pounds? How much should you give if you choose to give? Part of the culture of Islam is that people help others, you'll notice people begging from the locals outside mosques. So, you could set aside an amount of money to give to those people who you feel you want to support.

We only encountered aggressive begging once, at a set of traffic lights in Meknès. Around the big cities you will see sub-Saharan Africans positioned at traffic lights and roundabouts waiting for the lights to change or a queue to form. They will then go from vehicle to vehicle asking for money. We found ourselves at the front of the queue and we didn't have any cash to hand, so we didn't open the window and instead gestured that we didn't have anything to give. The beggar then started knocking more and more loudly on the window until it was rattling, then he started banging on the side of the motorhome. We grabbed the camera and pointed it at him, and he switched to hiding from the camera. We were very relieved when the lights finally changed. After that incident, we made sure we slowed down before we reached traffic lights that were red, so we didn't find ourselves in the same situation, and always has some small change to hand.

There is one area we feel we should offer our thoughts on when it comes to begging, and that is the child beggar. You will with certainly be begged from by children, asking for pens (*stylos*), sweets (*bon-bons*), a Dirham coin (*un Dirham*), a football (*un ballon*), clothes (*vêtements*), and so on. Bear in mind that unless there's been some extreme weather conditions in very remote areas, these children are very unlikely to be starving.

Child beggars in the road. Previous generations of motorhome owners have conditioned these little guys to expect gifts

If you give to them, even a small thing or a small amount, it can sometimes be more than their parents earn spending their hours working the fields. The message this sends to children is that begging is a profitable way to live, and must reduce their motivation for the difficulties they will endure in school and in trying to find a job afterwards. It also places a burden on follow-on travellers to do the same, as if they don't the children's expectations will not have been met, with unpredictable results. Think very carefully before giving to children: are you doing it with their future best interests at heart?

Sexual Harassment

In a country where female virginity at marriage remains of utmost importance, sexual frustration in young Moroccan men is to be expected. Anecdotal evidence abounds of Western women being constantly badgered and pestered by Moroccan men, but we have seen no evidence of this in practice. Marriage retains a higher status in Morocco than in the West, and women are expected to be accompanied at all times, either by a man or other members of their family, so a woman out or travelling alone will raise questions.

Women are also expected to adopt a strict dress code when in public, covering all but their hands, face and hair, and not wearing any tight-fitting clothing. One blogger who complained of being constantly chatted up by her guide in the desert subsequently posted photos of herself on a camel wearing tight, short hotpants and a strappy top.

While we can't condone harassment of any kind, you can help yourself by not being naïve. Even if you're in the heavily tourist-populated areas, where these rules seem more relaxed, take note of how the local ladies dress and act accordingly.

Dog Fear and Fascination

If you have a pet dog with you, it's likely to attract some attention when you take it for a walk. The reaction to your dog, it seems, depends on what your dog looks like. If they're small and cute, most children will be fascinated, and you'll come across them staring, trying to build up the courage to come and stroke them. Our dog is easy going so we'd encourage them to stroke his back gently, some would, and some daren't.

Kids interested in our dog in the Ziz Gorge

Larger dogs, and in particular black ones, invoke far greater fear in children and they keep their distance. This isn't surprising, there are lots of dogs living wild in Morocco, or being used as guard dogs for flocks of animals or premises. Local dogs have very hard lives, so we'd often carry a stick with us in case a guard dog took a dislike to our dog. If you don't have a stick and see one approaching, bend down as if to pick up a stone, they will usually back off as they have had a lifetime of stones thrown at them.

Ask the Price First, Always!

In a hundred transactions you might get overcharged a few pounds once, and guess which of those transactions you're going to remember! We've found everyday Moroccans to be highly trustworthy individuals, who'll charge you a fair price and will never steal from you. But in any society you'll get a few bad eggs, who will overcharge you. To reduce the temptation for them, and to avoid any nasty shocks, make you always agree the price of goods or service BEFORE you agree to take them. It can get tiresome, and it feels like you're not being respectful to the vendors sometimes, but if you don't do it, you will eventually get stung.

> We stayed at Camping Oued Drâa just north of Zagora for a night and were the only motorhome there. We had got used to campsites charging what is stated in the *Campings du Maroc* book and *campercontact.com* and there being a price list somewhere to confirm that. So, we forgot to ask the price before we pitched up. The following day when we went to pay, the owner doubled the price stated in the current Camping du Maroc book. We checked he knew we'd only stayed one night and told him the price in the latest campsite guide book but he smiled and said yes, the price has gone up. Always ask the price first, or you may find it's just 'gone up'.

The Hard Sell

Moroccan salesmen are masters at getting you to part with your money. From the simple, 'look no buy' to get you into their shop, or telling you that are lucky to be in town today as it's a jewellery festival (as it was the day before, and the one before that), to the elaborate, and mint tea accompanied, carpet shop pitch. In this latter one, not to be missed, numerous carpets are unravelled before you are asked to point to the ones you don't like so they can be taken away, leaving you with the one you like the best that you will obviously want to buy. The tactics are many and legendary. You will find them being deployed on you at some point in your stay. The only advice here is that even if it gets uncomfortable, the hardest Moroccan salesman can't force you to buy something you don't want.

Carpet sellers in Fes

The False Friend

You're walking down the street when a man with a pushbike says hello. He's going in your direction, and asks a few friendly questions. How are you? Where are you from? Ah, England, London? Manchester? Maybe he has a relative who's worked in the UK, or he's been there himself, and he tells you about them. You might ask him a few questions, does he live here, and is it always this hot? And on you go for half an hour before reaching a junction. He suggests you go right, that is the fastest and best way back to your campsite. You've already been here a couple of days, and you know left is the way to the campsite. He tries again a couple of times to save you from the 'longer' journey, and eventually says something along the lines of "but if you come this way I can show you around my shop". Boom. The false friend. It's a bit disheartening, but it's not malicious, shake his hand, touch your hand to your heart, tell him *bessalama* (bye!) and head off left. Unless you fancy looking round his shop.

Motorbike Guides

Driving into some major cities, particularly Fes in our experience, you may find yourself with a moped wing man, zooming alongside and trying to get your attention whenever you stop. These guys are paid to get motorhomes to visit whatever campsite they're attached to, and can be very difficult to shake off. The second time we visited Fes, a moped appeared and pulled alongside us at a roundabout. Knowing what was coming, we stopped the motorhome, opened a window and engaged in conversation with the moped rider. We told him we already had a campsite and we didn't need him, in French. No Moroccan tout worth his salt would be put off that easily, but as the traffic started to build up behind us, and we repeated our conviction we weren't following him. We didn't move our van to release the traffic until he eventually gave up and smiled, we shook hands through the window, wished each other a *bonne journée* (a good day, pronounced bon shoornay) and parted company.

The False Breakdown

This one's almost legendary, and although we've chatted with a British couple who fell victim to it in the past, it is so well known that now it almost never happens. You're driving off down some remote road, which is also relatively busy with motorhome traffic (for example the Drâa Valley). There's a car by the road with the bonnet up, and a man stood with an empty water bottle flagging you down. You stop and he asks for a lift to his village down the road to get help, leaving his friend with the car to take care of it. You invite him in, and 3 hours later find yourself trying desperately to get rid of the guy after he's taken you to three shops and a restaurant, all of which he gets a kick back from, while his mate's waiting somewhere nearby in his fully-functioning car. We've opted to take a hard-nosed approach of not stopping for locals who've apparently broken down, especially those who don't try to flag down the local cars that are passing.

Kif – Drug Dealers in the Rif

The Rif Mountains to the north of Morocco produce rather huge amounts of cannabis and kif, a mixture of hashish and tobacco. The drugs are all illegal to grow, sell, export, use or own, but all of these clearly go on (not just in the Rif Mountains, across Morocco, but it was the most visible to us there). The main explanation seems to be the fact the Rif is a historically poor area, and removing the most profitable business without replacing it with something equally profitable just isn't palatable.

> On our second day in Morocco we were driving on the N2 from Martil to Chefchaouen in the Rif Mountains. At a twisting section of road we kissed wing mirrors with an oncoming lorry, but no damage seemed to be done so, like the lorry, we carried on. Shortly afterwards a 4x4 overtook us, put its hazard lights on and pulled into a lay-by, waving us in. Thinking we may have damaged the lorry, we pulled in, alongside the 4x4 rather than behind it. The driver came to our window and said something, when we didn't understand he made a smoking gesture. Being utterly naïve we assumed it wanted a cigarette, so we apologised and told him we didn't have any because we don't smoke. He nodded OK, and we drove off, only later realising we'd been pulled over by a friendly, laid back drug dealer.

Tipping and Baksheesh

This one's as much a general confusion as anything. We read that tipping and baksheesh (small bribes), are a way of life in Morocco, and the line between the two is blurred. We'd often see small amounts of money being handed discretely between individuals, for no obvious reason. It was clear to us that tips were appropriate for Western-style services like restaurant waiters, petrol station attendants and taxi drivers. What was less clear was things like paying people in return for being allowed to take a photo of them, so we generally avoided that kind of thing. Although we read and heard something about the endemic corruption within Morocco's official institutions, we never saw any of this directly and it seems that tourists are not subjected to the same rules as the locals.

Photo Sellers

This is most prolific in the weird and wonderful Djeema el-Fna in Marrakech. This square is an ancient place in which story tellers, sellers of potions, henna tattoo ladies, shoe shiners, acrobats, monkey handlers and snake charmers congregate and make money from tourists; Moroccan, European, Asian, all of us. If you come to Morocco and only visit Djeema el-Fna, you'll have experienced Morocco in the same way as if you visit the USA and only go to Times Square in New York. You may find yourself subject to some dodgy practices, where prices are suddenly elevated beyond all reason – remember to always ask the price first.

> Walking through Djeema el-Fna with a friend, we were approached by a few men holding snakes. Our friend allowed them to be draped across his shoulders, and we took a couple of photos with our camera. The whole episode took about 3 minutes, and they insisted our friend now owed them 300Dh (about £24). He offered them a smaller sum, at which point they became aggressive and started to shout at him. He shouted back, and in among various obscenities coming back our way we walked off feeling threatened and upset.

False Museums

In some places establishments, whose primary aim is to sell items such as fossils, advertise themselves with large signs stating 'museum'. They're not museums in the way we know them, as the 'exhibits' are for sale. They are simply shops.

Stone Throwing

Children in Morocco sometimes throw stones at motorhomes. The French call it *caillassage*. We've personally only had it happen once, just a small pebble as far as we know, and no damage was done. Fellow travellers reported small numbers of such incidents too. Why the children do it isn't clear. It seems unlikely to be anything personal towards motorhome travellers, but it is upsetting if it happens. The advice we had was to keep a camera handy and point it at the children if you see them picking up stones. Just the threat of being photographed and those photos being shown to the police, who take such things seriously, is enough to deter.

Hand Gestures

We had a few young and teenage boys give us rude hand gestures. Why, we don't know, personal amusement perhaps. Our approach to this was to feign ignorance, smile and wave back at the finger-flickers. Some young and teenage girls blew kisses at us, which was a much nicer gesture.

Taxi Scams

We've not used many taxis in Morocco but there are anecdotal stories of a few scams which taxi drivers try to pull off on green tourists, especially in the cities like Marrakech. Look out for petite taxi drivers claiming the meter is broken or declaring they have no change at the end of your journey, obliging you to give them a larger note.

Theft

We've kept this one to last because it just doesn't seem to be a problem for motorhome travellers in Morocco. We had no issues with theft, and we never met anyone who did. However, we would still recommend taking precautions such as not visiting city centres at night, not carrying much cash, not flashing around money or jewellery, parking in official places with guardians if possible, and keeping valuables close in busy city streets. As with any heavily touristed area in the world, there is always the possibility of pick pockets, so be extra vigilant in the big towns and cities.

Our Routes

Morocco is a big country, and we know as an independent traveller you'll want to follow your own nose. The following sections show the routes we took around the country in 2012 and 2017, and later on we give a rough idea of where we went and what there is to see. We've given motorhome-specific information about some of the places we found the most inspirational, fascinating and beautiful.

2012

Our 2012 route was roughly based on ones used by some guided tour operators, and took in many of Morocco's 'bigger' sights. We did it in a month, which provided enough time but did require some drives of 4 or 5 hours a day. We wrote blog posts as we travelled with photos, videos, prices and so on, so you can get much more information on each of the locations below. To see these posts, either click on the icons on our map (*tinyurl.com/ourtourmap*) or go to our first day's blog post for this tour at *ourtour.co.uk/home/africa-were-in* and use the arrows to move to the later days.

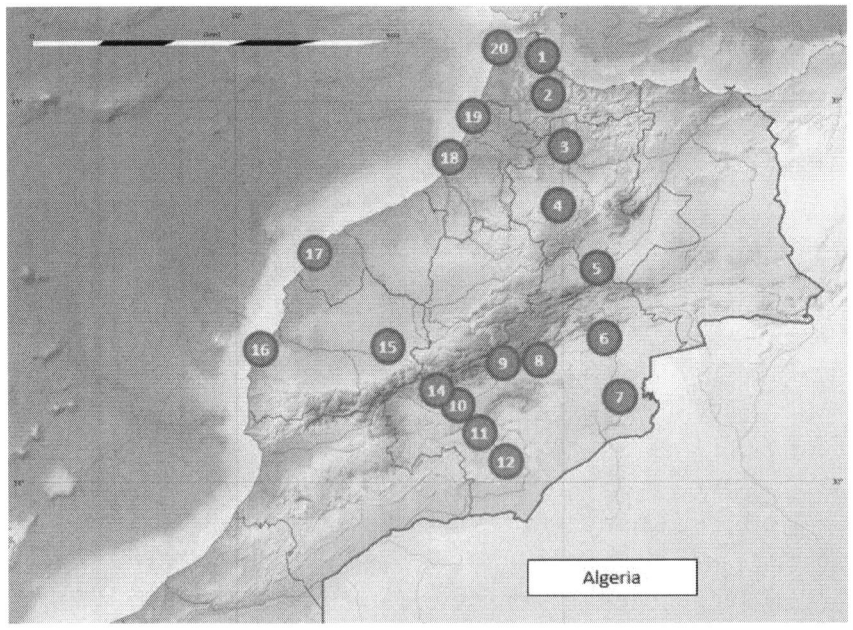

Our one-month tour of Morocco

As you can see by following the numbers on the map below, we travelled clockwise around the country, heading down through the Rif Mountains (1 and 2) to Fes (3), over the Middle Atlas from Azrou to Midelt (4 to 5) and then down to the Sahara at Erg Chebbi (6 and 7). There we backtracked north and west to the Todra and Dadès Gorges (8 and 9). We then swung south at Ouarzazate (10) and travelled down the Drâa Valley to Zagora (11 and 12). Retracing our route back up the Drâa Valley to Ourzazate again, before visiting Aït Benhaddou (14), then over the Tizi-n-Tichka pass to Marrakech (15). From there we took to the coast at Essaouira (16), and used some of the fast motorway network to head north via Oualidia (17), Kenitra (18) and Moulay Bousselham (19). Finally we stayed at Tangier (20) before leaving from Tanger Med.

The locations we visited are indicated with numbers on the map, below is the name of where we stopped and GPS co-ordinates:

1. Martil, Camping Complexe Touristique Alboustane (GPS: N35.62890, W5.27736)
2. Chefchaoeun, Camping Municipal Azilan (GPS: N35.17567, W5.26715)
3. Fes, Camping Diamant Vert (GPS: N33.98718, W5.01847)
4. Azrou, Emirates Euro Camping (GPS: N33.44339, W5.19094)
5. Midelt, Camping Municipal de Midelt (GPS: N32.67778, W4.73704)
6. Meski, Camping Source Bleue de Meski (GPS: N31.85714, W4.28347)
7. Erg Chebbi, Auberge Tombuctou (GPS: N31.12817, W4.01261)
8. Todra Gorge, Camping Le Soleil (GPS: N31.54747, W5.59090)
9. Dadès Gorge, Hotel Kasbah de la Vallee (GPS: N31.52107, W5.92985)
10. Ouarzazate, Camping Municipal de Ouarzazate (GPS: N30.9230, W6.88678)
11. Agdz, Camping Kasbah de la Palmeraie (GPS: N30.71208, W6.44610)
12. Zagora, Camping Auberge Prends Ton Temp (GPS: N30.33777, W5.83219)
13. Ouarzazate, Camping Municipal de Ouarzazate (GPS: N30.92322, W6.88731)

137

14. Aït Benhaddou, Guarded Parking in Kasbah Car Park (GPS: N31.04221, W7.12982)
15. Marrakech, Camping Manzil La Turtue (GPS: N31.61473, W7.88949)
16. Essaouira, Camping Sidi Magdoul (GPS: N31.49183, W9.76303)
17. Oualidia, Guardian Parking near Lagoon (GPS: N32.73229, W9.04387)
18. Kenitra, Camping De La Chenaie (GPS: N34.25692, W6.56787)
19. Moulay Bousselham, Camping Caravanning International (GPS: N34.87528, W6.28817)
20. Tanger, Camping Miramonte (GPS: N35.79092, W5.83273)

2017

Our 2017 route went anti-clockwise around the country. We wrote blog posts as we travelled, so you can see what the roads were like, the campsites, food and so on. Again, you can access the posts using our map (*tinyurl.com/ourtourmap*) or by going to the first blog post for this tour (*ourtour.co.uk/home/africa-algeciras-assilah-morocco*) and clicking the arrows to follow the tour.

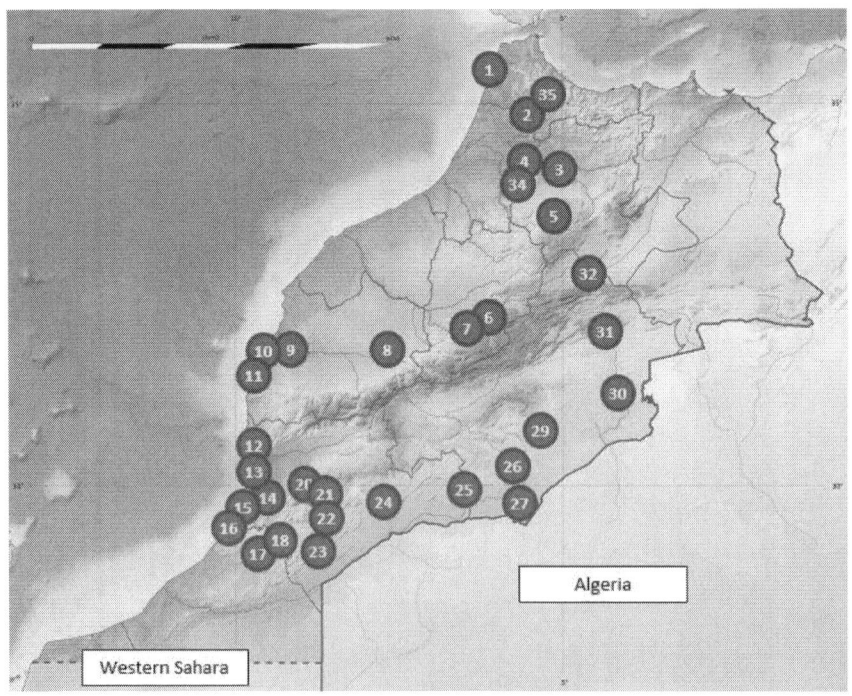

Our three-month tour of Morocco

Referencing the map below, we started off at Tanger Med, staying the first night at Asilah (1). From there we headed inland to Fes (3), breaking the journey just south of Ouezzane (2). From Fes we went west to Moulay Idriss (4), then south to Azrou in the Middle Atlas Mountains (5). Here we stayed west of the Middle Atlas, travelling south to a campsite near the dam at Bin-el-Ouidane (6), and then onwards to the waterfall at Ouzoud (7). Next we took the road to Marrakech (8), and then, like in our first tour, we headed for the coast at Essaouira (10), staying overnight at the small town of Ounagha (9) on the way. From Essaouira we stayed on the Atlantic coast, taking in Sidi Kaouki Beach (11), Taghazout (12), and Sidi Rabat (13).

From Sidi Rabat we nipped inland to Tiznit (14) before heading back to the coast at Mirleft (15) and Sidi Ifni (16). Here we decided this was about as far south as we wanted to go, and turned back inland to Abaynou (17) and Bouizakarne (18) and back up to Tiznit (the 19th location – shown as 14 on the map). The famous road east up into the Anti-Atlas Mountains brought us to Tafraoute (20). Staying in the Anti-Atlas, we slept at the painted rocks near Tafraoute (21) and then the Aït Mansour mountain oasis (22). Here we took an amazing but awful quality road south (which included 30km of rough piste!) to Icht (23). Shadowing the border with Algeria, we headed east to Tata (24) and Foum Zguid (25) and on to Zagora (26). After a detour to watch the nomad festival in M'hamid (27), we turned north, again this time stopping near Zagora (28 in list, shown as 26 on the map) and then heading east to Tazzarine (29).

Next up we retraced our 2012 steps, visiting Erg Chebbi (30) and the Ziz Gorge (31) before crossing the High Atlas Mountains and staying near Midelt (32). The Middle Atlas Mountains and the cedar forests took us back to Azrou (5), and from there we headed first to Mèknes (34), then the blue town of Chefchaouen in the Rif Mountains (35) and finally we left Morocco again at Tanger Med.

The locations we visited are indicated with numbers on the map, below is the name of where we stopped and GPS co-ordinates:

1. Asilah, Camp As Saada (GPS: N35.471942, W6.02888)
2. Ouezzane, Camping at Motel Rif (GPS: N34.772705, W5.544475)
3. Fes, Guarded Parking – not available for overnight stays as of 2019 (GPS: N34.060933, W4.985881) and Camping Diamant Vert (GPS: N34.06093, W4.98588) – which was closed for several months in 2019 but now appears to be open again
4. Moulay Idriss, Camping Zerhoun Bellevue (GPS: N34.0147, W5.561628)
5. Azrou, Emirates Euro Camping (GPS: N33.443252, W5.190994)
6. Bin-el-Ouidane, Camping L'Eau Vive (GPS: N32.106487, W6.479088)
7. Ouzoud, Camping Zebra (GPS: N32.004948, W6.72035)
8. Marrakech, Guardian Parking (GPS: N31.624023, W7.996325) and Camping Ourika (GPS: N31.52754, W7.95944)
9. Ounagha, Camping des Oliviers (GPS: N31.53174, W9.54774)
10. Essaouira, Guarded Parking next to medina – as of 2019 it is no longer possible to overnight here (GPS: N31.51087, W9.76642)
11. Sidi Kaouki, Beach Camp Sidi Kaouki Beach (GPS: N31.35108, W9.79493)
12. Taghazout, Camping Terre d'Ocean (GPS: N30.56292, W9.74094)
13. Sidi Rabat, Hotel La Dune (GPS: N30.08633, W9.66371)
14. Tiznit, Camping Riad Tiznit (GPS: N29.6955, W9.7084)
15. Mirleft, Semi-Official Guarded Parking (GPS: N29.59033, W10.03689)
16. Sidi Ifni, Camping El Banco (GPS: N29.38263, W10.17627)
17. Abaynou, Camping De La Vallee (GPS: N29.11414, W10.0199)
18. Bouizakarne, Camping Tinnougba (GPS: N29.18637, W9.72785)
19. Tiznit, Camping Tazerzite (GPS: N29.64332, W9.72252)
20. Tafraoute, Municipal Parking Area (GPS: N29.7232, W8.98559) and Camping Granite Rose (GPS: N29.71729, W8.98437)
21. Painted Rocks, Free Camping (GPS: N29.6649, W8.97296)
22. Aït Mansour Gorge, Guardian Parking (GPS: N29.5479, W8.87746)
23. Icht, Camping Borj Biramane (GPS: N29.05896, W8.85184)
24. Tata, Camping Hayat (GPS: N29.73845, W7.9776)

25. Foum Zguid, Camping Khayma Park (GPS: N30.08024, W6.87198)
26. Zagora, Campsite Oasis Palmier (GPS: N30.32389, W5.82649)
27. M'hamid, Hamada du Draa Auberge Campsite (GPS: N29.82112, W5.72009)
28. Ternata, Camping Oued Draa (GPS: N30.40687, W5.86999)
29. Tazzarine, Camping Amasttou (GPS: N30.77488, W5.56212)
30. Erg Chebbi, Auberge La Chance (GPS: N31.13488, W4.01594 and Kasbah Mohayut (GPS: N31.131684, W4.015469)
31. Ziz Gorge, Camping at Hotel Jurassique (GPS: N32.15366, W4.37646)
32. Midelt, Ksar Timnay Camp (GPS: N32.75249, W4.91963)
33. Azrou, Emirates Euro Camping (GPS: N33.443252, W5.190994)
34. Mèknes, Guarded Parking (GPS: N33.889871, W5.565713)
35. Chefchaouen, Camping Azilan (GPS: N35.1756, W5.26701)

Ideas for Places to Visit

The Atlantic Coast

Also see **Asilah** in 'Entering Morocco: From Spain to Your First Night Stop' section earlier in this book.

Essaouira, Mirleft and Sidi Ifni

The Atlantic plays host to some chilled-out towns where you can spend a few days in the sunshine and enjoy beaches, rolling waves and easy-going hospitality. We've grouped together a few towns under this heading, but they each have a different history and feel to them. They're all easy to visit in a motorhome.

Essaouira

Pronounced ess-a-wee-ra, this coastal town is within an easy drive of Marrakech down the N8 and the R207, with about half of the drive on fast, dual carriageway. As ever be aware that speed cameras will be pointed your way! Being so easy to get to (you can get cheap flights from the UK to Essaouira), the town's pretty busy with tourists, and as a result it does have a few touts knocking about. Those guys aside, the town's working fishing port (bring a nose peg), beach and medina are all attractive and fascinating spots to kill some time.

The Essaouira medina

We visited Essaouira twice, the first time stopping in the campsite to the south of town, Camping Sidi Magdoul (GPS: N31.49167, W9.76333), and the second time in one of the town's guarded parking locations by the medina walls (GPS: N31.510871, W9.766425). Our friends stayed at one of the other guarded parking locations just to the south of the town, near the dunes, and reported it to be a better option (GPS: N31.49563, W9.76369), although the guardian did tend to ask for a *cadeau* 'gift' from those staying. As of 2019 none of these locations are available for overnight stays, and most motorhomers seem to be visiting for day trips before staying in out-of-town campsites.

> The touts at the seafood restaurants in Essaouira, off Place Moulay Hassan, went into overdrive when we looked for one to eat in one evening. They were frankly obnoxious, more so than those in Djeema el-Fna in Marrakech. Even at the restaurant we chose (stall number 10), the owner upped the agreed price when we came to pay afterwards, requiring some stern words before he relented and reluctantly gave our change back. Essaouira has a well-deserved reputation for being laid back, but you might want to avoid these eateries if you want to really enjoy the place.

Scarves for sale in Essaouira

Mirleft

Further south down the coast, below Tiznit, you'll find the small seaside town of Mirleft. Again this has a reputation for being low hassle, and we found that was definitely the case for us. It was far less touristy than Essaouira, probably as it's a work-a-day kind of place with no real attraction as such, but for some nice coves.

We stayed in one of these coves at a semi-official guarded parking area (GPS: N29.590328, W10.036889). The place proved too popular and the following day the police arrived and politely asked the motorhomes not to stay overnight, as they had received complaints that locals could not access the car park for the beach. Some friends opted to stay anyway, and were not bothered by the police again, and some moved to the small Camping de Nomads site in the town itself and reported it to be good (GPS: N29.57992, W10.04368).

Semi-official motorhome parking near Mirleft

Sidi Ifni

Further south again you'll find hundreds of fellow motorhome travellers in the campsites along the estuary mouth and coastline at Sidi Ifni, a surfing spot not too far north of the Canary Islands. We opted for Camping El Banco (GPS: N29.382631, W10.17627), mainly as the other sites were packed. Once installed on a sea facing pitch we enjoyed the open sea view and sunsets, but did find that if it got too windy our motorhome got covered in sea spray.

The town is on a cliff behind the campsite, so it's a steep-ish walk up the steps or streets but worth it for the wonderful views of the site and sea from the promenade above. Again Sidi Ifni is short on big sights, but the general feel of the small fixed market area and cafés is relaxing and fun. We killed a few days watching the surfers, eating out and cycling the nearby roads.

A park in Sidi Ifni

Camping El Banco facing the Atlantic in Sidi Ifni

Bird Watching in Moulay Bousselham or the Souss-Massa National Park

Even if you're not an ornithologist, these two coastal bird watching locations were great places to visit.

Moulay Bousselham

This small town has a couple of campsites. We stayed at Camping International (GPS: N34.87528, W6.28817), which got slighter better reviews and is up against an inlet to the coastal lagoon where the birds are found, albeit separated by a fence. Small fishing boats gather nearby selling their catches, and locals will approach you to offer tours of the bay in their boat.

Bird watching in Moulay Bousselham

We haggled a little for a couple of hours on the water. Our guide brought along binoculars and a bird identification book, and was clearly passionate about the birds and seemed to us very knowledgeable. Back at the campsite we found they would deliver plates of hot chips direct to our van, which won our hearts! The town itself wasn't much to look at, but we used Moulay Bousselham as a way to break up a long coastal motorway journey.

Souss-Massa National Park

The tiny village of Sidi Rbat (or Sidi Rabat), about two hours south of Agadir, wasn't on our radar at all until a French couple recommended it to us. This beautiful spot, a short walk to the beach, is quiet but for the crashing Atlantic rollers. It's on the edge of the Souss-Massa nature reserve, an easy walk away, and famous as home to one of the world's rarest birds, the Bald Ibis (which you'll need a guide to find). As well as the nature reserve, there are fishermen's caves built into the cliffs above the beach, well worth a walk down to take a look at. We stayed on an official area for motorhomes on a flat piece of land opposite Hotel La Dune (GPS: N30.086328, W9.663707).

The hotel parking was easy to reach, on a paved road except for the last section through the village which is piste, but easily passable in good weather. You pay at the hotel for the parking and the cost includes use of a shower and toilet block inside the hotel compound. There's a good restaurant on site too, we recommend the fish tagine, and they can also organise guided tours of the nature reserve. The only issue we had was one of the hotel staff was a bit too persistent in his requests for any alcohol we might have.

Motorhome parking outside Hotel La Dune in Sidi Rabat

Inland Towns and Cities

Also see **Chefchaouen** in 'Entering Morocco: From Spain to Your First Night Stop' section earlier in this book.

The Imperial Cities – Fes, Meknès and Marrakech

Morocco's Imperial cities of Fes (also written as Fez) and Meknès are well worth your time and effort to visit, and no trip to Morocco would be complete without seeing Marrakech.

Fes

The UNESCO-listed Fes medina is simply incredible, something you're unlikely to have ever seen before. Walking through one of the high arched *babs*, the old city gates, is the closest thing we can imagine to being transport backwards in time by hundreds of years. A thousand years of Moroccan culture are crammed into the space of the twisting streets, not forgetting the famous tanneries. The buildings and monuments are gracious but clearly slowly decaying, although we saw signs of renovation in 2017, with new metal doors being replaced with traditional wooden ones.

Fes tannery

While it feels at times you're on a film set, and the streams of people and donkeys are laid on just for you, look a little closer and you'll see the place remains a living, working city. With around 9400 alleyways, the medina would take weeks to really get to know.

Visiting Fes by motorhome is as easy as you want to make it. You can use the A2 toll motorway to approach the city from the south, taking the easy 201 road almost to the entrance of the most popular of the city's two campsites, Camping Diamant Vert (GPS: N33.987852. W5.019011). Safely ensconced in the campsite, you can arrange with them for an official, licensed guide who will, for only £10 or £15 a head, drive you into and around the city, spending a few hours walking you through the medina, showing you the Royal Palace and taking you to a view point above the city.

If you want to get a bit more up and close and personal with Fes, there is a large official guarded parking location (GPS: N34.060933, W 4.985881), close to the blue gate entrance to the medina, Bab Bou Jeloud. This involves driving into the city, but on new, wide roads which are easy to navigate. Right at the end you have to drive through an archway, take care at this point as it has a traffic light on the other side, which some cars choose to ignore. The guardians will wave you into the parking area. If you can, park alongside the walls so you feel less exposed! As of 2019 police are reported to be visiting this area at night and instructing motorhomes to move to one of the city's two campsites.

The walk into the medina takes minutes, so you can enter and leave as you want to. The general advice is not to go deep into the medina at night, as you might meet a few nefarious characters. During daylight hours the place is safe and the hassle from sellers, restaurant touts and faux guides relatively low, but take the usual precautions against pickpockets.

Daytime guardian parking in Fes, close to Bab Bou Jeloud

Meknès

Meknès felt in some ways like a mini version of Fes. While the medina is no comparison, the city does have its own Royal Palace and the mausoleum of Sultan Moulay Ismail, which was closed for redevelopment in 2017. The Meknès campsite closed some years ago, but there are a couple of official guarded parking locations in easy walking distance to the medina. We used the shared car/motorhome parking just outside one set of the city walls (GPS: N33.889871, W5.565713), which was busy with maybe 30 motorhomes when we visited. The sugar cane drinks being freshly crushed by the vendors on the short walk to town were delicious, if teeth-threatening.

The square in Meknès, the guarded parking is just out of shot to the left

Marrakech

You could spend days in Marrakech and still not see everything. But while it has plenty of other outstanding sights to see, Djeema el-Fna, the main square is the part of the city which sticks in our minds and you'll likely leave loving or hating the place. UNESCO summarised what makes it special: "The spectacle of Jamaa el Fna is repeated daily and each day it is different. Everything changes — voices, sounds, gestures, the public which sees, listens, smells, tastes, touches. The oral tradition is framed by one much vaster — that we can call intangible.

The Square, as a physical space, shelters a rich oral and intangible tradition." In other words, the square is a pretty mad, ancient, frenetic and fun place to be. It changes nature between night and day, and every day is different as new characters arrive and others leave.

Story tellers love being photographed in Djeema el-Fna (for a not so small fee)

The atmospheric and frenetic evening food stalls in Djeema el-Fna

Visiting Marrakech by Motorhome is as easy as Fes. There are several good quality campsites on the outskirts, which you can reach without driving into the city centre. We stayed at two of them: In 2012 at Manzil la Tortue, 12km to the east of the city off the N9 (GPS: N31.61473, W7.88949). This was a great quality site, not cheap by Moroccan standards but worth it. The owners offered a taxi service which dropped us off near Djeema el-Fna and picked us up again at an agreed time in the evening. The only issue with the site was about 2km of piste which had be driven to get to it, which we didn't relish after four and a half hours crossing the Tizi-n-Tichka High Atlas Mountain pass, nor did we enjoy fending off the children begging from us on the piste.

Orange juice – a low cost way to get a seat to watch the Djeema el-Fna action close up

The second site we used, in 2017, was Camping Ourika on the P2017, again about 12km from the city centre this time to the South. Another good quality site, with a restaurant, pool and a view of the snow-capped High Atlas from the gate. Taxis into the centre could be arranged by the campsite reception, but we opted to drive in and to stay at the official guarded parking because we were running in the half marathon which closed many of the roads around the city.

The Marrakech guarded parking is just a stone's throw from Djeema el-Fna and the action in the medina. It's located just behind the famous Koutoubia mosque, and is well enclosed and protected by both high walls and guards and there is electric hook-up available if you want it (GPS: N31.624023, W7.996325). The price was similar to a campsite, but seemed to us very reasonable considering where we were, and we stayed several nights on two separate occasions.

Top Tip: the Djeema el-Fna square gets very busy on Saturday nights, and the Marrakech guarded parking fills up with cars. The cars are double-parked, blocking in the motorhomes, but the hand brakes were left off so the guardians could push them back and forwards to enable other cars to arrive or leave. If you intend to arrive on a Saturday don't leave it too late arriving and if you want to leave on a Saturday night it would be best let the guardians know in advance.

Guarded parking in Marrakech, behind the Koutoubia Mosque and a stone's throw from Djeema el-Fna

The Berber Market and Barbary Apes in Azrou

Azrou's set in the Middle Atlas Mountains, and is an easy going and authentic introduction to modern Berber life. There are no campsites or overnight guarded parking locations in the town centre, but the incongruous, castle-themed Emirates Euro Camping (GPS: N33.443252, W5.190994) is only about 3km to the north of the town. We've used this campsite three times, and it offers a clean, safe and hassle-free haven for the frazzled traveller.

We strongly recommend timing your visit to Azrou so you can take in the Tuesday Berber souk, which you can drive to and park outside among the many lorries, trucks, motorbikes and donkeys, or walk/cycle to. Head towards the town on the N8, then take the road to the right 1km from the campsite, just before the N8 bends to the left and heads downhill. The souk spreads out over a vast area and sells pretty much everything from fruit and veg, to animal feed, household goods and fabrics.

There are also large tents selling mint tea and snacks, but they aren't for the faint-hearted. Meat is cut off carcasses hanging up in the tent and then minced, spiced and cooked while you wait, then served stuffed into bread rolls with extra spices. If you get to the souk in the morning, you'll be rewarded with the sight of the large animal market, mainly consisting of hundreds of sheep in small herds being traded and hauled around.

Sheep for sale in the weekly Azrou souk

If you want to go and see some of Morocco's Barbary Apes in the wild, there are a few nearby locations, you can find them on this website *www.morocco-knowledgebase.net/tim/azrou-monkeys.jpg*. To get to one of them in the nearby Cedar forest (GPS: N33.4263947, W5.1555147), turn right out of the campsite entrance and head north on the N8 for about 500m, then turn right and follow the road for another 4.5KM or so. There's a guarded car park at the end, and various tourist shops.

A Barbary Ape near Azrou

Top Tip: Coming south from Fes or Meknès to Azrou, the onwards journey south on the N13 takes you over the Middle and High Atlas Mountains, and down to the wonderful Sahara desert at Erg Chebbi. Alternatively you can take the N8 south-west towards Marrakech, but be warned if you take that route you'll have a long drive (4 to 6 hours) to find any official stopovers.

An Ordinary Town with Extraordinary Hospitality – Bouizakarne

Bouizakarne to the east of Sidi Ifni doesn't have much to attract the passing motorhome tourist, with the exception of the outstanding family hospitality at small, new Camping Tinnougba (GPS: N29.186373, W9.727855). The site's located on a flat desert plain about 3km from the centre of town and along about 1km of easy piste from the tarmac road. The site has little more than a tiny (but very well kept) toilet and shower block, a water tower/kitchen and a single wall, to hold back the frequent winds which blow across the dry, open plain.

Reports from fellow travellers drew us in, of a warm welcome from the Berber family who own, run and are gradually building the site from nothing. On our arrival we found the reports to be accurate, and enjoyed speaking English and French with the owner and his son, getting some insight into life as a Moroccan.

The friendly and welcoming owner of Camping Tinnougba near Bouizakarne

The Atlas Mountain Ranges

Waterfall in the Middle Atlas - Cascade d'Ouzoud

The waterfall (cascade) in **Ouzoud** is 110m high and a popular day trip from Marrakech. If you're coming from Marrakech, the best road is the R208 and then the R304, both of which we were advised have better views and are devoid of traffic compared with the N8.

The campsite we used, Zebra Camping, is about a 1km walk from the waterfall. The site was well established, having been created from the bare ground up by a Dutch couple over the previous 10 years. The restaurant has character and the tagines on offer had novel ingredients and were well worth a try. We enjoyed the view from the site for a couple of days, taking a walk down to the waterfalls through the town.

The falls themselves aren't huge but worth the walk, although if you want to see them from the bottom be aware you'll have to run a gauntlet of tatty tourist shops and cafés.

Cascade d'Ouzoud)

Outstanding Landscapes in the Anti-Atlas – Tafraoute and the Painted Rocks

The Anti-Atlas Mountains towards the south of Morocco present a landscape like nothing you're likely to have ever seen. The slopes around, laid down over millennia, have long ago buckled upwards and eroded, leaving a huge 'combed' look to the hills and mountains. In broad creases between the rock lie oasis towns, a steady reminder of the wonderfully exotic part of the world you're rolling through.

Driving through the Anti-Atlas Mountains south of Tafraoute

Tafraoute

Our friends described the town of Tafraoute, in the south-west part of the Anti-Atlas range, as like being in an episode of the Flintstones. Huge orange rocks bake in the sun, for all the world appearing as though they've been made from *papier mâché* for an epic film version of the cartoon. Tafraoute has a reputation among motorhome travellers as being a fantastic destination. Partly driven by the 360-degree beauty of the landscape around you, partly by the laid-back Berber town itself, and partly by the ease with which you can camp there. The dramatic scenery on the R104 from Tiznit over the Kerdous Pass is an attraction in itself.

The town has three official campsites, made up of small walled compounds overflowing with motorhomes into the surrounding oasis. By far the largest population of motorhomes, 200 or more in the winter months, are located outside the formal campsites in a municipal parking area which charges around 10Dh (80p) a night to stay. This area has open views of the countryside, has no marked out locations and allows camping behaviour. A tanker drives the site each day delivering fresh water for a small cost, and bins placed in the centre of the site removed rubbish periodically.

Hundreds of motorhomes in Tafraoute, the Valley of the Vans

The Tafraoute municipal parking area would be quite perfect but for the fact there is no black waste disposal, and a steady stream of motorhome owners walk or drive their quad bikes to the edge of the site each day to dump raw sewage. There's no need to do this, you can drive or walk to the nearby Camping Granite Rose and empty waste there in a dedicated disposal facility for a just couple of quid. Unhappy about the constant flow of people dumping their black waste, we only stayed a couple of nights in the municipal area (GPS: N29.723201, W8.985595), before moving to Camping Granite Rose (GPS: N29.717286, W8.984369), both a short walk into the town.

Tafraoute has a number of leather shoe makers gathered together in the town, you can't miss them, where you can buy traditional *babouche* (slippers, pronounced bab-oosh) for 80Dh (about £6), hand-made, custom leather boots for 200Dh (about £16) or leather sandals for 60Dh (about £5).

Collecting made-to-measure leather boots in Tafraoute

The Painted Rocks

While in Tafraoute we recommend you take the opportunity to go and see the famous *rochers peints*, the painted rocks. They're about 12km from the town, and at first we cycled to them on the R107 from the town, before driving the same route and staying overnight at our only free camping place in Morocco (GPS: N29.664898, W8.972959). The last mile or two (depending on where you plan to stay around the rocks) are on piste, but it was easily passable during good weather. There were a handful of other motorhomes staying above the rocks with us, and many more down alongside the rocks in what appeared to be an established and tolerated free-camping location. We spotted people getting water from a tap next to a gate leading to the only fenced off area around.

The normally orange rocks are painted in a faded blues and reds

The piste road to the painted rocks

High Atlas Mountains -
The Tizi-n-Tichka, Aït Benhaddou and the Atlas Film Studios

The Tizi-n-Tichka
Heading north from Ouarzazate, the N9 gradually works its way upwards into the sky, over the High Atlas Mountains via the Tizi-n-Tichka pass and then back down again to Marrakech. The road has a good surface, is wide, kept free of snow and has crash barriers. There are slow-moving lorries crawling along with hazard warning lights flashing on the steeper uphill or downhill sections, but if you take care when overtaking them, and allow plenty of time for the journey you'll cross the pass with ease.

Atlas Film Studios
Heading north, before you reach the pass, there are a couple of tourist attractions which we enjoyed. The first is on the N9 at Tamassinte, the Atlas Corporation Film Studios, where parts of epics like The Jewel of the Nile, Gladiator and The Living Daylights were filmed. Gradually eroding film sets are shown to you by the official guide included in the ticket price, and you generally get the opportunity to have a lot of fun.

A set at the Atlas Film Studios north of Ouarzazate

Aït Benhaddou
25km further north, about 9.5km (6 miles) north of the N9 on the P1506 (a sealed road), you'll find the Aït Benhaddou ksar, an old fortified village, very picturesque, and now better known as a living film set and tourist destination. When we visited in 2012, we parked by the La Kasbah Hotel (GPS: N31.04221, W7.12982). As of 2019, the Nouflla campsite gets good reviews on *park4night.com*, with views over the ksar a short walk away (GPS: N31.040745, W7.127550).

Top Tip: There's no need to use a guide to look around the ksar, unless you want one. It's not huge and is relatively easy to navigate by yourself, but a local guide may be able to give you more information on local life, and which areas were used in which films.

Aït Benhaddou

Gorges

The Anti-Atlas Mountain Oasis of the Aït Mansour Gorge

The Aït Mansour Gorge seems to be little-visited by motorhome tourists. Why, we don't know, as it's a magical place, a mountain oasis set within a deep-sided orange gorge. The drive from the R107 was narrow in places, but good quality sealed road, and was itself spectacular. As you arrive in the Aït Mansour Gorge the palm trees appear and you quickly reach the palm-shaded guarded parking area, which Mustapha and his wife Fatima have looked after for some years (GPS: N29.547902, W8.877461).

Guardian parking at Aït Mansour

There's a restaurant close to the guarded parking and a café about a kilometre further down the gorge, but the main attraction is the scenery and view of life in a mountain oasis. You'll be rewarded with jaw-dropping views if you walk or cycle about 4.5km (3 miles) down the gorge to a fantastic view point on the road (GPS: N29.5307067, W 8.8511904).

Top Tip: We drove the full length of the gorge in our motorhome after Mustapha told us we could do so and drew a road on our map for us. We turned to the right at the end of the gorge, near Souk-el-Had-d'Afella-Irhir, and headed west on a sealed road, not shown on the Michelin map, to the R107 about two miles north of Izerbi. Both the drive through the gorge, and the road to Izerbi, were through quite incredible scenery, never to be forgotten drives.

Driving through the Aït Mansour gorge

The Todra and Dadès Gorges

Running along the southern side of the High Atlas, the N10 has a couple of well-known, and well-frequented gorges running up to the north, the Todra and Dadès Gorges. You can drive the most scenic parts of both gorges on tarmac, but if you continue on either road up further into the mountains, the road quality deteriorates to piste, and most two-wheel drive motorhomes will need to come back down again to the N10.

Dadès Gorge

The Dadès Gorge is famous for a photo you can take from a café at the top of a short series of hairpin bends, about 28km (17 miles) north of the N10. Unless you're heading into the hills to the north, these hairpins are the most difficult part of the drive, and they'll be easy for most motorhomes. The terrace for the café at the top has the monopoly on the view of the road, so is a little more expensive than usual. We ate a tagine there with friends in the sunshine, looking down over the hairpins and into the gorge, which was a memorable experience.

The Dadès Gorge

During our visit to Dadès in 2012, we opted to stay in the gorge itself, in the car park opposite the La Kasbah de la Vallee hotel (GPS: N31.52107, W5.92985). By taking a meal in the hotel, they allowed us to stay overnight free of charge, but the hotel is now offering a formal camping service. *Campercontact.com* is currently showing six campsites in the gorge, so there's plenty of choice.

Driving down the Dadès Gorge

Todra Gorge

The Todra Gorge is famous for a short section of steep-sided canyon, through which a concrete road runs carrying tourist buses and other traffic. It's a pretty sight, but there will be tourist stalls in the gorge, a tat-gauntlet to navigate your way through to the far side which offers opportunity for walking or climbing. We stayed at Camping Le Soleil in Tineghir, for two nights (GPS: N31.5476, W5.58915), and drove up the gorge, parking outside a mosque before walking up to the narrow section.

The Todra Gorge

The South and the Sahara Desert

The Desert Ring Road – Icht, Tata and Foum Zguid

The N12 from Icht through Tata to Foum Zguid runs through *hamada*, stony desert, parallel with the Algerian border about 20 miles to the south. While the scenery isn't as spectacular as the routes through the Anti-Atlas to the north, it's a great road to drive. We were held up by wayward camels, fascinated by the *pisé* (mud brick) walls and buildings alongside and within lush oases, and thoroughly warmed through by the bright light of the Saharan sun.

Icht

In Icht we stayed at Borj Biramane, a small French-built and run tourist complex on an area used long ago for camel trains to rest up after crossing the desert. The site is a hotel with a large area geared up for motorhomes (GPS: N29.058956, W8.851843), and had very good quality facilities. While the sun beat down, we relaxed under our awnings, floated in the small pool, ate succulent take-away brochettes from the site restaurant, got four loads of washing done and dried for us, and made the odd foray into Icht by bike. The campsite also organises tours of the old town where some families still live underground.

Tata

Tata held us for longer than Icht, and we struggled to dislodge ourselves from the river-side site at Camping Hayat, about 500m from the town (GPS: N29.7384469, W7.9776043). The town of Tata is much larger than Icht and offers a good array of shops and restaurants. With almost no hassle from vendors or touts, it felt like an easy place to be and the town's oasis was a pleasure to cycle through.

Tata from above

Metal workers in Tata

Foum Zguid

Next along the N12 to the east Foum Zguid is a tiny town sometimes used as part of the gruelling Marathon des Sables, with an array of shops and cafés. We used the town mainly as somewhere to rest, staying in the unkempt Camping Khayma Park (GPS: N30.080244, W6.871981), 800m from the centre of town. Friends who also stayed in Foum Zguid cycled to a new campsite just outside the town and opted to stay there instead as they felt it had better facilities. As we only stayed a couple of nights, one of which was spent having an evening campfire and a glass or two of wine with fellow German and French travellers, we didn't bother to move. From Foum Zguid, the now-tarmacked N12 takes you all the way to Zagora in the Drâa valley.

The N12 to Foum Zguid

The Drâa Valley to the Sahara – Agdz, Zagora and M'hamid

The Drâa is Morocco's longest river, although most of the time only part of the 680-mile riverbed has any water in it. Heading south from Ouarzazate, the N9 climbs upwards and before you reach Agdz presents a spectacular view back to the north and into the surrounding hills. From Agdz down to Zagora it's all about palm trees and kasbahs. All along the route you'll spot plenty of both.

Agdz

In the small town of Agdz we stayed in Camping Kasbah de la Palmeraie in 2012 (GPS: N30.7121596, W6.4455013), a fairly basic campsite but with the advantage of having a *palmeraie* and *kasbah* on the premises. We paid for the tour (in English) of the kasbah and found it to be very good, as was the tagine that we had delivered to our motorhome for tea. All money raised by the campsite and tours goes towards the restoration of the kasbah.

The Kasbah at Camping Kasbah de la Palmeraie in Agdz

Zagora

We stayed in Zagora in both 2012 and 2017, first in Camping Auberge Prends Ton Temp (GPS: N30.33772, W5.83220), and the second time in Camping Oasis Palmier (GPS: N30.32301, W5.82492). The former was closer to the town but very small. It had good facilities and a restaurant where the owner and his friends played an informal gig after our meal. The latter is about 5km (3 miles) from the centre of Zagora but is set under the palms with great walks into the *palmeraie* and up the Jebel Zagora hillside opposite.

Again, the site had good facilities and a good restaurant and if we were to stay in Zagora again, we would probably return here. In the town, keep an eye out for the famous '52 Days to Timbuktu' sign (GPS: roughly N30.3234234, W5.8410468), although it gets moved around and repainted from time to time, it's still fun to get a photo alongside it like Michael Palin.

The famous 52 Days to Timbuktu sign in Zagora

The desert landscape seen from a walk up Jebel Zagora near Camping Oasis Palmier

M'hamid

From Zagora it's a couple of hours slog south into the Sahara Desert, or at least as close as you can get to it on this route, as the road runs out at M'hamid (or Mhamid). The road was generally in good condition in 2017, although it was in the process of being upgraded so sections of it were piste, the longest being about 10km long. We stayed at the Hamada du Drâa auberge campsite (GPS: N29.821122, W5.720088), reputed to be the best in town. It didn't disappoint, especially as it was right next to the camel racing course (the dry Drâa river bed), which was part of the annual International Nomads Festival!

A nomad in M'hamid

The campsite is surrounded by high walls, which offer welcome relief when the wind picks up and wafts the sand around. It is built around a small hotel with a pool and good restaurant, campers use the shower and toilet facilities in the hotel. The shower water is pumped into the plants around the campsite every morning, leaving a grey water smell for a couple of hours a day, but as water is so scarce it seems a very sensible thing to do – and most motorhomes took the opportunity to add their grey water to the plants at the same time.

Small dunes in M'hamid. If you want the big ones, you need a 4x4

From M'Hamid, if you want to go see the big sand dunes of Erg Chigaga, you're going to need a 4x4 tour to take you 35 miles west, which the campsite will happily arrange for you. People who we spoke to who took a tour really enjoyed it. They stopped overnight in a Berber tent and hunted for fossils, but the main reason they enjoyed it was because the dunes weren't as busy as the dunes at Erg Chebbi.

Parked Alongside Saharan Dunes – Erg Chebbi

Erg Chebbi is Morocco's other Saharan Erg, but unlike Erg Chigaga near M'hamid, you've no need to rent a 4x4 to visit the dunes, you can park up right next to them. After navigating the dire roads in Rissani (in 2017 they looked like they were being resurfaced, but we think they were in a similar state in 2012) we headed south down the well-surfaced N13. In 2012 we had to drive a couple of kilometres of piste to reach the dunes at Auberge Tombuctou (GPS: N31.12817, W4.01261). This is a three-star hotel with pool, spa and restaurant, where we hooked-up to a palm tree-mounted socket and could see camels sleeping a hundred meters away, with the orange sand dunes just beyond them.

Auberge Tombuctou at Erg Chebbi

By the time we returned in 2017, a road had been built from the N13 to the dunes, so only very short sections of piste were needed to get to the many campsites and auberges offering camping along this stretch of road. This time, spoiled for choice, we stayed in a couple of places, the best of which by far was the dune campsite at Haven Auberge La Chance (GPS: N31.13488, W4.01594), complete with unspoiled views, a pool, and camel or quad bike tours into the desert, a simply incredible place to stay in your motorhome.

Having fun in the dunes at Erg Chebbi

Thanks very much for buying our book, we really appreciate it and hope it inspires you to head off and enjoy the big wide world. If you have enjoyed the book or found it useful, please take a moment to leave us a review on Amazon. These really help other readers and give us feedback too on how we can improve later editions.

About the Authors

Julie and Jason Buckley quit work just before they turned 40 in 2011, to take a once in a lifetime, one-year tour of Europe in their motorhome. Documenting their travels on their blog *ourtour.co.uk,* two years later they finally returned home. Yearning for more adventures, they set a goal to change their lives and become financially free, enabling them to travel whenever they wanted to.

Aged 43, they 'retired' and took to the road once more to explore from the North Cape in Norway to the Sahara Desert in Morocco. They now mix up their time between motorhome life and their base in Nottinghamshire, England. Julie and Jason have written several books to help and inspire others to follow their own motorhome dreams or to start their own journey to financial freedom.

As they travel Julie and Jason write about their experiences on their blog:

www.ourtour.co.uk

While this book focusses on the practical side of travelling to Morocco, some of the additional stories, photos and videos available on the blog might also be of interest. There are over a thousand posts and pages on the blog from all over Europe and North Africa, you may want to get started here:

- The first Morocco blog post for our 2012 tour: *ourtour.co.uk/home/africa-were-in* (here's a shorter URL if you need to type it in: ***tinyurl.com/n5w972h***)
- The first Morocco post for our 2017 tour: *ourtour.co.uk/home/africa-algeciras-Asilah-morocco* (***tinyurl.com/llyegou***)
- To see an interactive map of places we've visited, with each place linking to the blog post about it, go here: ***tinyurl.com/ourtourmap***

Other Books by the Authors

The Motorhome Touring Handbook
Packed full of practical advice from choosing a motorhome and touring the UK to travelling abroad or planning for and enjoying a year-long tour.

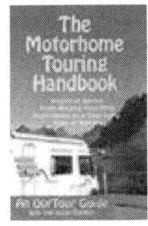

The 200
200 of the most memorable, fun, varied, inspirational and interesting places we've stayed, in over a decade of motorhome touring.

A Monkey Ate My Breakfast
A travelogue of our first motorhome tour of Morocco in 2011, an eye-opening adventure onto a new continent, and into a new and exotic culture.

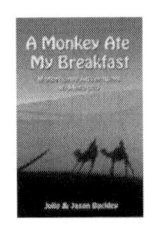

Motorhome France
A helping hand for anyone wanting to take their motorhome across the channel for the first time to explore this motorhome friendly country

OurTour Downloaded
All the blog posts from our first year of full-time motorhome touring, handily gathered into one ebook

The Non-Trepreneurs
A practical guide explaining how we think about and manage our personal finances to enable us to retire aged 43, and travel whenever we want.

Reference Information

British Embassy in Rabat

British Embassy in Rabat - *www.gov.uk/government/world/morocco*. Note that these should only be used in the event of a serious issue, such as being attacked or arrested. They can't deal with passport issues; check their website above for more advice.

Address:
28 Avenue S.A.R. Sidi Mohammed, Souissi 10105 (BP 45), Rabat, Morocco

Email rabat.consular@fco.gov.uk
Telephone: +212 (0) 537 633 333
Fax: +212 (0) 537 758 709

Office hours: Monday to Thursday, 0800-1615; Friday 0800-1300 Consular public opening hours: Monday to Friday, 0800-1200 – an appointment is required.

Ramadan Opening Hours: Mon to Thurs, 0800-1400; Friday 0800-1300.

Useful Websites

The following websites (among others) were consulted during the writing of this guide.

A useful and insightful English language blog of a Canadian lady living in Morocco - *marocmama.com*

An English language motorhome forum dedicated to Morocco - *forums.motorhomefacts.com/135-morocco-touring*

French language forum for taking a motorhome to Morocco – useful for a whole range of topics – registration is free and it translates fairly well with Google Translate but some maps are only available after you've created several posts on the forum - *www.maroc-campingcar.com*

Another French language forum for motorhome travel in Morocco - *www.ccomaroc.com/forum*

Official UK government guidance for taking a pet abroad - *www.gov.uk/take-pet-abroad/overview*

UK NHS advice for travel to Morocco - *www.fitfortravel.nhs.uk/destinations/africa/morocco.aspx*

Information about the new GHIC card, the replacement for the EHIC: *www.nhs.uk/using-the-nhs/healthcare-abroad/apply-for-a-free-uk-global-health-insurance-card-ghic*

UK Foreign Office advice for Morocco - *www.gov.uk/foreign-travel-advice/morocco*

Dogs and Islam - *www.animalsinislam.com/islam-animal-rights/dogs*

Literacy rates in Morocco 2015 - *www.moroccoworldnews.com/2015/10/170473/illiteracy-rate-in-morocco-decreases-to-32-percent*

Recycling in Morocco - *www.worldbank.org/en/news/feature/2016/02/16/morocco-lets-nothing-go-to-waste*

The UNESCO listing for Fes medina - *whc.unesco.org/en/list/170*

A good article on kif in Rif Mountains - *www.journeybeyondtravel.com/blog/kif-rif-hashish-morocco.html*

Motorhome rental in Morocco - *www.zigzagcamper.com*

Arabic Phrases - *www.speakmoroccan.com*

Printed in Great Britain
by Amazon